Trading in oil futures and options

Trading in oil futures and options

Sally Clubley

CRC Press
Boca Raton Boston New York Washington, DC

WOODHEAD PUBLISHING LIMITED

Cambridge England

Published by Woodhead Publishing Limited, Abington Hall, Abington
Cambridge CB1 6AH, England
www-woodhead-publishing.com

Published in North America by CRC Press LLC, 2000 Corporate Blvd, NW
Boca Raton FL 33431, USA

First published 1998, Woodhead Publishing Ltd and CRC Press LLC
Reprinted 2004
© Woodhead Publishing Ltd, 1998
The author has asserted her moral rights.

British Library Cataloguing in Publication Data
A catalogue record for this book is available from the British Library.

Library of Congress Cataloging in Publication Data
A catalog record for this book is available from the Library of Congress.

Woodhead Publishing ISBN 1 85573 387 0
CRC Press ISBN 0-8493-0519-5
CRC Press order number: WP0519

Printed by Lightning Source, Milton Keynes, England

Contents

Preface

This book is intended as an introduction to price risk management in the worldwide oil industry. Although primarily aimed at those new to risk management it will also serve as useful background theory to those with more experience and will show those in other markets how the oil industry uses futures and other derivatives.

It looks at the history of the oil industry and how it developed to a stage where futures markets became an inevitability. The futures exchanges were followed in the late 1980s by the development of the over-the-counter markets and the oil industry now has a whole range of risk management tools enabling everyone from crude oil producer to refined product consumer to find the necessary instrument. This book looks at both the theory of futures, exchange options and over-the-counter trading and also the practical applications for the oil industry.

Tight controls will, of course, be maintained throughout any trading activity. It is a relaxation or absence of control, often combined with a lack of understanding at all levels of a company, which has led to almost all the major losses immortalised in popular futures market history. A risk management policy stating exactly what the company wants to achieve with any hedging activity should be drawn up and compliance with it ensured. There are few companies who could not then benefit from judicious use of risk management.

The oil industry of today is completely different from that of twenty years ago: the challenges facing it can only increase as markets de-regulate throughout the world. An understanding of price risk management will be an essential part of any company's or individual's ability to face these challenges.

Sally Clubley

The development of the world oil industry

Origins of the modern oil industry

Until the middle of the nineteenth century the world had little interest in crude oil. Its existence had been known for centuries; it had been found seeping out of rocks in biblical times and afterwards, but its usefulness, particularly as a fuel, was never really appreciated. It was treated in the same way as tar and primarily used for waterproofing purposes.

The real origins of the modern oil industry are in Pennsylvania, where Edwin Drake made the first commercial discovery of crude oil in 1859. He is generally acknowledged to be the first person specifically to drill for, and find, crude oil. Very quickly he was followed by others, both in Pennsylvania and elsewhere. The first oil rush resulted in the discovery of large amounts of crude oil, initially in the US, and led swiftly to the first oil glut and a fall in price more dramatic than any seen since, with prices dropping from $20 per barrel in 1860 to 20 cents per barrel only a year later.

Oil refining was, in fact, a technique already in use when Pennsylvania's first oil was drilled. Some ten years earlier, a plant had been built in Scotland to process the shale oil seeping into coal mines

1

in the area. But the small-scale project failed to attract any real interest and refining can really be said to have started with the treatment of the American oil. Initially, uses had to be found for the new oil products. Oil lamps were soon prevalent in oil-producing regions and lubrication developed as another major application in the early years. Within a very short time, oil had begun to establish its almost unassailable position as an essential fuel source and raw material in the industrialising world, particularly after the development of the internal combustion engine. But the political and economic upheavals that oil would cause a hundred years or so later were still unthought of as the race to find more black gold continued.

By the turn of the century the United States and Russia, still ranked second and third in the world today, were already established as the world's leading oil producers, thus beginning a domination that was to last until the large producers of Venezuela and the Middle East combined forces under the banner of OPEC in the mid twentieth century.

Oil was first discovered in the Middle East in the early part of the twentieth century but it was not until many years later that production in the Arabian Gulf (then, as now, the cheapest area of production in the world) got underway. The first oil well in the Middle East can still be seen in Bahrain.

The major oil companies

In the late 1920s and early 1930s a race developed to capture the largest number of drilling rights in the Arabian Gulf – an area rich in oil deposits but offering largely hostile conditions and lacking the technological ability to develop them. The runners in this race were the major oil companies, known as the 'Seven Sisters', of which six still exist. These companies, despite intense competition and bitter arguments, operated effectively as a cartel, dominating the oil industry until the 1960s. It was only in the last decade or so of the twentieth century that their influence began to wane.

Five of the Sisters were American; three of them (Exxon, Mobil and Chevron) the offspring of one corporation – John D. Rockefeller's Standard Oil Company. Rockefeller was one of the first people to recognise the importance of integrating oil company activities and keeping control of the oil at the drilling stage, through refining, distribution and delivery into the consumer's oil tanks. The company dominated the US oil industry and, by implication, the world's markets but it was eventually disbanded by legislation in 1920. The group splintered into around forty separate companies, each operating in one state. Of these, those in New Jersey (Exxon), New York (Mobil) and California (Chevron) became the most important. The other two US Sisters, Gulf, taken over by Chevron in the 1980s, and Texaco both began life in Texas, which still plays a vital part in the US oil industry with a large proportion of the crude output and refining capacity, many pipeline terminals, landing ports and trading companies. Rockefeller had been excluded from Texas from the beginning and never managed to gain a foothold in the state where North America's greatest oil reserves to date were found in the late nineteenth century.

The remaining two Sisters were both European – British Petroleum and Royal Dutch/Shell. The latter was formed by the amalgamation of two companies: one Dutch, one British. The growth of both of these Sisters was based on oil reserves far from home – BP in Iran and Russia; Shell in Venezuela.

These seven companies completely monopolised the industry until the 1960s; drilling for, producing and refining the crude, distributing the products and, finally, retailing them to the consumer. As the oil potential of the Middle East became apparent, the companies formed a series of consortia (after much battling among themselves) to negotiate with the local governments and rulers and arrange production deals. The Middle Eastern governments at that time had no complaints; they were simply happy to see their income growing.

Outside the seven, the only company that achieved any degree of success was the French national oil company, Compagnie Française de Pétrole (CFP). This was admitted into consortia that were involved in Iran and Iraq, though not at the very beginning. It was not until CFP discovered oil independently in Algeria that it was really ranked as a major oil company.

From the beginning the industry was faced by a major problem: transportation. (Shell, in fact, developed from a shipping company but found itself struggling to survive until it merged with Royal Dutch.) Outside North America oil was being produced many miles from the areas of demand – in Venezuela, Mexico, the Arabian Gulf and Russia. There existed a number of agreements among the Seven

Sisters to exchange oil, in order to prevent the transportation costs becoming too much of a burden. All posted (i.e. official) crude oil prices in the early twentieth century were based on a theoretical price in the Gulf of Mexico plus transport costs, so these exchanges could be quite advantageous to the companies concerned.

The detailed history of the world's oil industry has been well chronicled elsewhere but some brief notes are necessary for an understanding of the current state of affairs and likely future developments.

The oil industry in the twentieth century

In the early part of the century it seemed that all sides of the industry were reasonably content with the way things were going. The producer countries were well paid for the use of their resources; the oil companies were all enjoying high profits and had plenty of oil reserves. After the Second World War the battle for a share of the market became the most pressing problem for the oil companies – oil demand was booming and no one wished to get left behind in the rush for expansion.

But already the signs of change were, in retrospect, becoming apparent. In the Middle East, the Gulf states and Iran had been using the income from oil to send their young men overseas for education and those returning from Europe and the United States began to question the situation whereby the producing governments had virtually no control over their own resources. The governments had, however, initiated costly and extensive development programmes that were dependent on continuing wealth and were wary of damaging their relationships with the oil companies.

The first move was made by Venezuela, which passed a law in 1948 requiring the oil companies to hand over 50 per cent of their profits. The companies, realising they had little alternative, agreed and the idea quickly spread to the Middle East, where it was taken up, with similar results, first by Saudi Arabia and later by others.

The resentment of the oil companies spread, especially with the gradual emergence of independent oil companies set up either by individuals like J. Paul Getty or by consumer government agencies such as Agip in Italy. At around the same time, too, CFP made its Algerian discoveries. These independents began to make production agreements with the producer governments, offering better royalties than the Sisters. This suggested to the producers that they were not being paid as much as they could be, and they began to consider ways of swinging the advantage towards themselves. The first concrete move came in the form of an alliance between Saudi Arabia and Iran. The terms were very loose, amounting to little more than a vague co-operation agreement, and had virtually no effect. Meanwhile, Venezuela was continuing an effort started some years earlier to persuade the producers to get together to form some sort of combined opposition to the multinational companies.

Throughout the 1950s, however, the status quo was maintained, with most of the producers coming to better agreements with the companies but otherwise leaving operations alone. One notable exception to this was Iran, which nationalised its oilfields in 1951. This move was followed by a western boycott of Iranian oil; a small sacrifice for the companies (apart from BP, which was very reliant on Iranian oil) because there was once more a glut on the world oil markets. Two years later, western governments intervened to bring down the revolutionary regime in Iran and re-establish a climate in which the Iranian oil industry could restart operations. Although the glut made the companies somewhat reluctant to increase production, the Iranians were in severe financial difficulties and it was essential, politically, that contact be made. At this stage the BP monopoly in Iran was broken and the Seven Sisters formed a consortium with CFP to continue the development of Iranian oil. Despite the fact that one company had suffered, it now seemed that control of the industry was firmly back in the hands of the seven major oil companies.

The next event of major importance was the Suez crisis of 1956, as a result of which the Arab states imposed an oil embargo on the west. Although the total world oil supply was hardly affected, because production was increased elsewhere, irreparable damage was done to the relationships between the producers and the oil companies, particularly the two European ones. Perhaps the main feature of the embargo was that it showed that the producers could act together when sufficiently aroused. In the aftermath of Suez, several of the smaller independents reached still 'better' terms with the producers, and further damage was done to the Seven Sisters.

Throughout this time, the oil glut was continuing. While it was in nobody's interests (except those of the consumer, who had little say in things) to reduce the price of oil, it soon became inevitable that this would happen. In 1959 the crude oil price was cut for the first time this century. The inevitability of the move meant that there was little real protest from the producers; but a meeting of the Arab Petroleum Congress quickly followed. The meeting produced no firm action. But, when the companies imposed a second price cut the following year, the Congress met again, this time with Venezuela in attendance, and the Organisation of Petroleum Exporting Countries (OPEC) was formed by Venezuela, Saudi Arabia, Iran, Iraq and Kuwait.

There was, however, no dramatic action from OPEC and everything carried on much as it had before. The group pledged co-operation to avoid 'unnecessary fluctuations' in the price of oil; but even so, the coming changes in the structure of the industry were still virtually imperceptible.

Oil demand was booming, production was increasing and incomes following suit: there was no reason for any conflict. Prices did not increase sharply, but rose gradually from $1.20 per barrel in 1960 to $1.80 a decade later. But the higher production levels kept the producers' incomes rising steadily. The only worry facing the industry was whether the oil reserves would last until the end of the century, but even this was of no real concern – reserves were increasing as new areas were being explored and drilled, and technology was improving, allowing more oil to be extracted from each well and enabling previously impossible reserves to be developed.

Perhaps the most significant change during the 1960s was the increasing part played by the major US oil companies in the European market, following the imposition of import controls by the US government in 1957. The US Sisters and independents had to market all their Middle Eastern, North African and other foreign oil outside the USA. The only real consumer market available was Europe, and oil companies launched into fierce advertising battles to increase market share and develop brand loyalty in the consumer, particularly in the fast-growing gasoline market. By the time the US import controls were lifted, the major oil companies had established lucrative European markets, where they remained active until the early 1980s when some withdrew altogether from the European retail market, to be followed by others as the market became less profitable.

Since the Suez crisis, when the oil boycott had been successfully executed, albeit with little effect, there had been some concern about an orchestrated move by the oil producers to block exports to the west

6

for political or economic reasons. But, by 1970, when the next move was made, many had come to believe that any concerted action was unlikely – the producers were thought to be enjoying their increasing wealth too much.

The oil price rises of the 1970s

In 1970, however, the Libyan government imposed reduced production levels on Occidental Petroleum, an independent oil company totally reliant on Libyan oil. The company's production was cut back by almost half, forcing it to agree to higher posted prices and an increased royalty for the Libyan government. At the semi-annual OPEC meeting at the end of that year, the ministers called for a 55 per cent royalty agreement for all member countries. Negotiations with the oil companies resulted in an acceptance of OPEC's terms, on the condition that, apart from an agreed increase to allow for inflation, there would be no new demands for five years. In 1973, however, the OPEC countries decided to impose a 70 per cent increase in prices. The announcement came during a boycott on oil supplies to the United States and the Netherlands following the Yom Kippur war. World supply was short and prices rose. By the end of 1973 the posted price for Arab light crude was $11.65 and the spot price more than $20 per barrel. Prices on the spot market, which at that stage handled only small amounts of oil left over from term contracts, had never before risen above the official price. Although the spot market tended to give a somewhat exaggerated picture, it gave a strong indication of the industry's fears.

During the same year Saudi Arabia, the largest producer within the cartel, obtained an improved participation agreement with the oil companies, not only for itself, but also for the smaller Gulf producers – Kuwait, Abu Dhabi and Qatar. The agreement gave the producers a 25 per cent equity in production, rising to more than 50 per cent in 1982. Libya had achieved a similar result by nationalising its oilfields and Iraq had taken over 100 per cent equity. In fact, further pressure from the producers led to a much faster takeover than originally planned, with several achieving 100 per cent equity by the end of the 1970s.

Consumers responded to the sharp price rises of 1973 by cutting back and demand slumped. Most continued to blame the oil companies for the increases, not as yet realising that they had all but lost control of pricing. These cutbacks were, however, short-lived. When the oil embargo was lifted in the middle of 1974, demand quickly began to rise again. This trend continued, even through the steady price rises of the next few years.

The Iranian revolution in 1978, and the subsequent war between Iraq and Iran a year later, was to bring about the second oil crisis of the 1970s. Immediately after the revolution oil production in Iran dropped sharply. Prices rose on the spot market, but it was some months before any increase in posted prices was imposed. But the real harm was not done until the beginning of the war. Iranian production had fallen from a peak of over 6 million barrels per day (mbd) in 1974 to 5.7 mbd in 1978 as the internal unrest grew. By the end of 1979 the country was producing little more than 1 mbd and Iraqi output fell from over 3.5 mbd to less than 1 mbd.

Although significant areas of production were being developed elsewhere, the industry was still walking a tightrope between supply and demand, and was unable to cope with such a large cutback in supply. Product and crude prices on the European and US spot markets more than doubled during the course of 1979. Day after day the price just continued to rise and any trader managing to get hold of oil was sure to make a profit. All logistical factors were forgotten as the scramble for oil continued.

In time, however, the sharp escalation in prices had a corresponding, though opposite, effect on demand. 'Free world' oil demand peaked at 51.2 mbd in 1979, fell to 48.6 mbd the following year and continued to drop, reaching 44.8 mbd in 1983, the lowest level for ten years. Cause and effect may be difficult to determine but the world recession following the high oil cost high inflation of the 1970s was undoubtedly the main reason for the fall. But the spin-offs – increased conservation and the switch to alternative forms of energy – have played a strong part and are to some extent irreversible. The exact effect of each cause remained difficult to measure as changes in industrial technology and improved energy conservation meant comparisons were impossible even when the world moved out of recession in the mid-1980s. One survey suggested that heating oil demand per house for space heating fell by around 40 per cent in Germany from its 1979 high, largely because of more efficient heating systems and better insulation.

After the 1979 crisis the OPEC members decided to introduce price differentials for their crude oils. Changing demand patterns had made the lighter North African crudes, for example, very much more attractive than the heavier Gulf crudes, which produced less gasoline and more fuel oil. Arab light crude, with the largest volume, was chosen as the marker, with premiums of up to $9 per barrel being paid for some of the better crudes and discounts being applied to the very low quality ones.

It was these differentials, rather than the actual price of crude oil, that brought OPEC close to collapse in the early part of 1983. A year earlier, the benchmark price had been lifted to $34 per barrel and the maximum differential cut to $3 in an attempt to halt the slide in oil prices seen in the spring of 1982, as production continued at high levels and demand kept falling. For a while it looked as though this attempt might have been successful.

Meanwhile, crude oil producers outside OPEC were gaining in importance, most notably the United Kingdom, Norway and Mexico. In 1973 three of the world's top five oil producers were in OPEC, but ten years later the United Kingdom and Mexico had displaced Iran and Libya, leaving only Saudi Arabia in the top five. In the first quarter of 1982 non-OPEC production exceeded OPEC output for the first time in twenty years. OPEC was becoming the swing producer. Table 1.1 gives a breakdown of world oil production figures between 1978 and 1996.

All these factors contributed to the worsening problems facing OPEC in the early 1980s when it met repeatedly in attempts to set price differentials between crudes, agree and monitor production levels and find other means of keeping control of oil prices.

Around this time both Norway and the United Kingdom decided to abandon the official pricing structure. Both countries moved towards a spot-related pricing system, which gradually became an actual spot price. The United Kingdom later abolished the British National Oil Company and all North Sea producers paid the government royalty direct, also on a spot-related basis. This led to an increase in the 'paper' trading of forward Brent cargoes as companies endeavoured to get the most advantageous price on which to base their royalty payment. This became known as tax spinning.

Although the OPEC countries maintained official price structures for a while longer than the North Sea, they ceased to have any importance and bore no relation to the actual prices paid by customers. The next few years saw great volatility in oil prices, with

Table 1.1 World oil production (000 barrels/day), 1978–96

	1978	1980	1982	1984	1986	1988	1990	1991	1992	1993	1994	1995	1996
Iran	5 275	1 480	2 410	2 195	2 060	2 335	3 255	3 500	3 525	3 700	3 710	3 715	3 715
Iraq	2 560	2 645	1 010	1 225	1 895	2 775	2 155	280	525	465	515	540	590
Kuwait	1 945	1 430	705	985	1 365	1 490	1 265	200	1 095	1 930	2 095	2 105	2 155
Saudi Arabia	8 315	9 990	6 695	4 760	5 210	5 720	7 105	8 820	9 100	8 960	8 875	8 890	8 920
UAE					1 595	1 620	2 285	2 640	2 510	2 445	2 480	2 505	2 600
Other Middle East	3 330	3 290	2 455	2 690	1 180	1 480	1 765	1 855	2 005	2 080	2 230	2 325	2 395
Total Middle East	**21 425**	**18 755**	**13 275**	**11 855**	**13 305**	**15 420**	**17 830**	**17 295**	**18 760**	**19 580**	**19 905**	**20 080**	**20 375**
Russia					11 305	11 440	10 405	9 320	8 035	7 155	6 420	6 205	6 075
Other FSU					1 100	1 155	1 180	1 150	1 110	1 025	980	1 010	1 085
Total FSU	**11 595**	**12 215**	**12 375**	**12 255**	**12 405**	**12 595**	**11 565**	**10 470**	**9 145**	**8 180**	**7 400**	**7 215**	**7 160**
USA	10 275	10 170	10 200	10 505	10 230	9 765	8 915	9 075	8 870	8 585	8 390	8 320	8 300
Mexico	1 330	2 155	3 005	3 015	2 760	2 875	2 975	3 125	3 120	3 130	3 140	3 065	3 280
Canada	1 575	1 725	1 485	1 645	1 805	2 000	1 965	1 980	2 060	2 185	2 275	2 400	2 460
Total N America	**13 180**	**14 050**	**14 690**	**15 165**	**14 795**	**14 640**	**13 855**	**14 180**	**14 050**	**13 900**	**13 805**	**13 785**	**14 040**
China	2 090	2 125	2 050	2 300	2 620	2 740	2 775	2 830	2 840	2 890	2 930	2 990	3 170
Indonesia	1 635	1 575	1 415	1 410	1 430	1 375	1 540	1 670	1 580	1 590	1 590	1 580	1 640
Other Asia Pacific	1 145	1 165	1 345	1 805	2 085	2 160	2 415	2 430	2 495	2 510	2 660	2 745	2 750
Total Asia Pacific	**4 870**	**4 865**	**4 810**	**5 515**	**6 135**	**6 275**	**6 730**	**6 930**	**6 915**	**6 990**	**7 180**	**7 315**	**7 560**
Algeria	1 230	1 120	1 045	1 075	1 195	1 250	1 345	1 345	1 320	1 325	1 310	1 325	1 395
Libya	1 985	1 830	1 135	1 105	1 065	1 060	1 430	1 540	1 475	1 400	1 430	1 440	1 440
Nigeria	1 895	2 055	1 285	1 385	1 465	1 445	1 810	1 890	1 950	1 985	1 990	2 000	2 150
Other Africa	985	1 170	1 320	1 640	1 720	1 955	2 100	2 145	2 185	2 215	2 245	2 340	2 500
Total Africa	**6 095**	**6 175**	**4 785**	**5 205**	**5 445**	**5 710**	**6 685**	**6 920**	**6 930**	**6 925**	**6 975**	**7 105**	**7 485**

Table 1.1 continued

	1978	1980	1982	1984	1986	1988	1990	1991	1992	1993	1994	1995	1996
Venezuela	2 235	2 235	1 965	1 875	1 885	2 000	2 245	2 500	2 500	2 590	2 750	2 960	3 145
Other S & C America	1 400	1 505	1 580	1 790	2 100	2 110	2 260	2 250	2 335	2 440	2 585	2 800	2 995
Total S & C America	**3 635**	**3 740**	**3 545**	**3 665**	**3 985**	**4 110**	**4 505**	**4 750**	**4 835**	**5 030**	**5 335**	**5 760**	**6 140**
UK	1 095	1 650	2 125	2 580	2 665	2 390	1 915	1 915	1 975	2 115	2 680	2 755	2 735
Norway	350	525	530	755	905	1 195	1 740	1 985	2 265	2 430	2 765	2 965	3 315
Other Europe	290	300	365	430	915	935	895	880	875	860	905	870	875
Total Europe	**1 735**	**2 475**	**3 020**	**3 765**	**4 485**	**4 520**	**4 550**	**4 780**	**5 115**	**5 405**	**6 350**	**6 590**	**6 925**
Total world	**63 050**	**62 745**	**57 060**	**58 105**	**60 585**	**63 270**	**65 720**	**65 325**	**65 750**	**66 010**	**66 950**	**67 850**	**69 685**
of which Opec %	**48**	**44**	**35**	**32**	**32**	**34**	**38**	**38**	**40**	**41**	**41**	**41**	**41**

UAE included in 'other Middle East' and FSU not separately shown before 1986; N America includes Mexico.
Source: BP.

13

OPEC meeting frequently but unable to prevent the fall in prices. However, predictions of its demise proved to be somewhat premature.

One of the most significant events of the next few years was the dramatic slide in prices in early 1986, when the price of West Texas Intermediate (normally seen as the benchmark of international oil prices since the success of the futures contract) fell to $9.75 per barrel. The fall followed the introduction by OPEC of 'netback' pricing: the crude oil price was determined by adding a margin to the prices received for the products after refining. Refiners' margin was guaranteed and they therefore had no interest in the level of product prices, selling all they could at any price.

OPEC then tried again to restrict production, with quotas allocated to each country. The next few years saw repeated arguments about the allocation of the quotas, with each country coming up with strong arguments as to why it should have its quota increased while all agreed that the overall total should be restricted. In the late 1980s and early 1990s production quotas were, more or less, adhered to and prices were helped by growing demand.

Changing price structure

While the market was seeing all these price changes a fundamental shift was taking place in the pricing structure. With the opening up of world markets and the looser integration of the majors the spot markets were increasing in importance. During the 1970s very little oil traded on the spot market, but through the 1980s this changed: the oil majors increasingly turned to the market as a regular source of supply, not just a means of obtaining barrels in times of scarcity and disposing of any excess. This in turn led to the growth of independent trading companies.

In August 1990 the oil industry faced its first major crisis for a decade: the invasion of Kuwait by Iraq's Saddam Hussein. Prices, as expected, soared as fears of supply shortages grew. For the next two months or so prices remained strong, but towards the end of the year they fell back to close to their pre-invasion level as it became clear that oil supply was still plentiful, despite an embargo on Iraqi exports and a lack of Kuwaiti crude. Early in 1991 the Gulf War began and prices remained more or less unchanged.

Fuel substitution and conservation patterns continued to have a major effect. It is clear that the recovery in the major economies in the mid 1980s led to a smaller increase in oil demand than many had expected, though the demand in the developing countries, particularly in South-East Asia, rose fast. A similar pattern was seen after the recession of the early 1990s, except that many of the South-East Asian growth rates had fallen to more sustainable levels.

Another feature of the market in the last decade or so has been the removal of government price controls in more and more countries. With the dismantling of the former Soviet Union and the introduction of market economies elsewhere, particularly in the Indian sub-continent and the Pacific Rim region, few governments now keep prices artificially low. In some cases prices are linked to historical oil prices, but increasingly retail markets are being released from control.

Gasoline markets have changed significantly in the last ten years or so. First, environmental concerns have meant there have been significant quality changes, notably the removal of lead and the introduction of less toxic products. The retail gasoline market, particularly in the UK and France, has also seen the arrival of non-oil companies. The oil companies have attacked the supermarket chains for selling gasoline at prices that do not reflect the full cost of production, distribution and retailing. Price competition has intensified and the UK in particular has seen the withdrawal of some of the majors. This trend may well spread into other countries.

The oil industry has also experienced many of the changes seen in other sectors. Increased monitoring of stocks and demand patterns has led to increasing use of 'just in time' deliveries: rather than hold expensive stock in tank refiners, distributors have been streamlining their systems so that crude or product does not arrive until it is needed. This has led to some sharp increases in price whenever supply is threatened, but these have generally been short term and there is no reason to suppose the policy will be changed.

The overall picture of the industry has also changed with OPEC countries investing heavily in downstream operations in the 1980s and 1990s and becoming virtually integrated oil companies. Some built their own refineries, others bought into existing refining and distribution operations in Europe and elsewhere, in many cases tying guaranteed long term crude supply to the deal.

OPEC members continue to hold more than three-quarters of proven oil reserves and will again exert some price domination in the future. But it seems unlikely that the cartel will ever hold together well enough to defy the international market. Oil prices seem likely to remain volatile and risk management to remain an essential part of the industry.

Oil refining

The refining process

Once produced, crude oil has to be refined to manufacture the various oil products and it is refining that provides the key to the oil industry. Although the basic principles of refining remain virtually the same, refinery technology has improved dramatically in the last thirty years. There are likely to be more alterations yet as the industry seeks to come to terms with the changes in demand that are forecast to continue beyond the end of the century.

Crude oil is a complex mixture of hydrocarbons, contaminated with sulphur, metals, salts and other compounds. The principle of refining is the application of heat to crude oil in order to separate the different constituents. A schematic diagram showing the way this is done in a simple hydroskimming refinery is given in Figure 2.1.

Gases

As heat is applied to the crude oil, different constituents boil at different temperatures and can be collected at various points in the

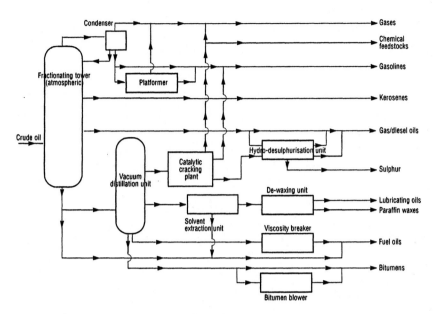

2.1 A simplified schematic diagram of oil refining.

distillation column. The temperature decreases as the oil moves up the column, so the compounds with the lowest boiling points, the gases, are collected at the top. The gases are primarily butanes and propanes, with some methane, ethane and other gases. They have a variety of uses ranging from chemical feedstocks to gasoline additives and bottled gas for domestic cooking and heating. Gases are a small percentage (usually 3–6 per cent) of the total yield from the heated crude oil.

Light gasolines

Collected at the next stage down from the gases are the light gasolines, which are used for the blending of motor gasoline. These account for only 5–10 per cent of the total yield. Gasoline is a mixture of chemical compounds and is blended to meet local requirements. High octane gasoline requires a higher proportion of naphthenes (also called cyclo-alkanes), which are made up of six- and five-membered carbon rings, than paraffins, or straight-chain carbon compounds. However, octane numbers can also be boosted by the addition of a variety of other compounds: lead used to be the main booster but has now been largely replaced by toluene and other aromatics and specially developed products such as methyl tertiary butyl ether.

Naphtha

Naphtha is the next product to be collected in the distillation column. This joins the light gasolines in the production of motor spirit. Both fractions are fed to a catalytic reformer, with butane and any other additives, for blending. Naphtha is also a major feedstock for the petrochemical industry in Europe, though not in the United States, where the LPGs (liquefied petroleum gases such as the alkanes) are preferred. There are differences, however, between the naphthas used for blending and those used for petrochemical production. The chemical industry prefers naphthas with a high paraffinic content, while the gasoline blenders like a high naphthenic and aromatic content. (The type produced in any particular refinery is determined by the crude used, not the type of plant.)

Naphthas account for a slightly higher proportion of the whole yield than gases and gasolines: usually 5–15 per cent.

Gases, light gasolines and naphthas are known as the light end of the barrel, because they consist of lighter hydrocarbons and are lighter in weight per unit volume than the other compounds.

Middle distillates

At the next stage of collection come the middle distillates, made up primarily of kerosenes and gas oil/heating oil. Kerosenes are mainly used as aviation fuel, though they also have applications as domestic burning and cooking fuel, particularly in the developing world, and for upgrading heavier products. In general, kerosenes are a fairly small fraction: usually 5–10 per cent of the barrel.

Gas oil, the heavier of the middle distillates, accounts for 25–35 per cent of the total. It has two major applications – space heating and diesel fuel. It can also be used by some European companies as a chemical feedstock in place of naphtha. Naphtha is preferred but, when the price differential widens, gas oil can become attractive. Not all European naphtha crackers have this capability to use gas oil, although those that do can have an effect on gas oil prices from time to time. Some smaller industries also use gas oil as a fuel source, but these are few.

Almost all middle distillate consumption demands a low sulphur content and this will be determined largely by the crude oil used. Middle Eastern and South American crudes, for example, tend to have a high sulphur content, while North African and North Sea crudes are 'sweet' or low in sulphur.

Residual fuel oils

Finally, when all the other products have been boiled off, some fuel oils are left. These are used for electricity generation and as industrial fuel and fuel for ships' bunkers (although some ships use marine diesel, a kind of gas oil).

Increasingly, however, these residual fuel oils are being used to feed upgrading facilities and to produce more light and middle distillate products. The sulphur concentration in residual fuel oil is higher than that of the crude from which it is produced because very little of it is removed during the distillation process.

Thermal cracking

There are three methods of upgrading residual fuel: thermal cracking, catalytic cracking and hydrocracking. The first to be introduced was thermal cracking, which works by the application of high temperatures at reduced pressure to increase the degree of distillation. The bonds between some of the carbon atoms are broken by the heat, leading to the formation of lighter products. The use of thermal cracking has been declining in recent years, partly because the newer technologies are more efficient and partly because the gasoline fractions produced do not meet today's requirements. As fuel economy becomes more important to the motor industry and the legislation concerning lead content increases, this decline is likely to continue.

Thermal cracking will certainly be used for some years in Visbreakers – the term used to describe the unit that reduces the viscosity of fuel oil by shortening the carbon chains within the molecules, thus making it easier to use and transport. The residual fuel oils can be so thick that they will not move in a pipeline, for example, until they are treated in some way.

Another form of thermal cracking was popular in Japan: residual fuel oil is heated until all the lighter hydrocarbons have evaporated and coke is left. The upgrading process is cumbersome and atmospherically unpleasant, but the equipment used for it is the cheapest type to install and operate.

Catalytic cracking
Catalytic cracking works on the same principle as thermal cracking but uses a catalyst to enable the treatment to be carried out at a lower temperature. It is not as effective as thermal cracking in increasing the middle distillates, but yields higher quality gasoline components. Vacuum gas oil is the ideal feedstock for catalytic cracking, but low sulphur fuel oils can now be used successfully. The equipment it requires is more expensive both to install and operate than for thermal cracking, but the higher value of the gasoline components makes it a more attractive investment.

During the late 1980s and early 1990s a large number of catalytic crackers were built, leading to an oversupply of gasoline for some time. They are likely to come into their own, however, as substitution continues to grow for non-transportation oil products and gasoline accounts for a still higher proportion of demand.

Hydrocracking
Chemically the most efficient upgrading process is hydrocracking. Hydrogen is added to residual fuel oil to increase the proportion of hydrogen atoms to carbon atoms and to produce more light constituents. This process is more flexible than either of the other two; its major disadvantage is cost.

Hydrogen feedstock for hydrocracking is normally expensive, making the plants costly to operate. These operating costs are around double those of a simple hydroskimming refinery, but gasoline yield is more than three times higher. Most hydrocrackers are currently situated near a cheap form of hydrogen supply, such as a chemical plant.

Changing patterns of demand and consumption

This refining of residual fuel oils in order to upgrade them was needed because of the changes in the demand for different products over the last twenty years. Gasoline demand as a percentage of all oil product demand has risen from 12 per cent in 1970 to around 29 per cent in the mid 1990s. There has been a significant change in demand for different grades of gasoline within that overall total, most notable being the shift from regular grades to premium and the increasing strength of low lead and unleaded gasolines.

Gas oil demand rose from 29 per cent in 1970 to around 37 per cent over the same period. Diesel cars and increased commercial road transport during the economic boom in the industrialised countries in the mid 1980s contributed to the good demand for gas oil. This continued into the 1990s as one in four new cars in some countries are diesel fuelled.

Fuel oil has lost market share over many years, dropping from 40 per cent of all products in 1970 to 17 per cent in the mid 1990s. The tendency is most pronounced in high sulphur fuel oil, which has very limited applications following the introduction of tighter environmental controls in many countries. Fuel oil is the only oil product that can be easily substituted (apart from gas oil's space heating demand) and many fuel oil consumers are now flexible in their feedstock requirements, capable of taking gas and, in some cases, coal as an alternative, making price the determining factor in demand.

Natural gas usage in particular has grown rapidly in recent years, accounting for almost 24 per cent of total energy consumption in 1996, up from 22 per cent in 1990 and less than 20 per cent in 1980. The rate of growth is likely to accelerate over the next decade.

In different geographical areas oil demand patterns vary considerably. The United States has traditionally been a high consumer of gasoline, which accounts for 42 per cent of total demand. This proportion has been more or less steady for the last few years. The fast-growing Asian market has seen gasoline's share increase to around 20 per cent. In Europe the gasoline share has fallen as the popularity of diesel cars has increased, largely due to a more favourable tax regime.

The change in demand has, of course, affected relative prices. The surplus of fuel oils kept prices low compared with other products through the early part of the 1990s. Gasoline prices recovered towards the middle of the decade after falling as increased production capacity came on stream a few years earlier.

Refinery economics have been under pressure for much of the last two decades. In 1996 consumption was around 90 per cent of total worldwide refinery capacity, one of the highest levels seen for some time. It took the refining industry a long time to recover from the demand falls of the late 1970s and early 1980s. The lead times in building a refinery are long and decisions on closure also have to reflect long term views.

There have been a number of years when refineries have lost money: variable costs, such as crude oil purchases, are almost always covered, but fixed costs may not be. Refineries tend to keep operating despite making losses because of the heavy depreciation costs suffered whether the refinery is operational or not. There are also strategic reasons, particularly for state-owned refineries, to keep operating.

In 1978 oil accounted for 53.3 per cent of total primary energy consumption in the OECD countries, but by 1996 this had fallen below 40.0 per cent. The main beneficiaries have been natural gas, nuclear energy and coal, illustrating one of the main problems with alternative fuel. All of these fuels substitute for fuel oil in power generation and space heating but not for the other major use of oil – transportation. As yet there have been no real alternatives developed for transportation that are both efficient and practical.

Some schemes, such as the Brazilian gasohol project where alcohol produced from sugar is added to gasoline, can be effective in a small area and when the circumstances are right. But in this case a plentiful supply of cheap sugar is essential and as the price of sugar increases it becomes a less attractive option. A similar project was looked at in the US Mid-West using corn as the alcohol feedstock, but this was rejected as economically unfeasible. Because of their use of agricultural products as feedstock, small-scale (in world terms) projects are likely to be initiated from time to time as politically expedient, but there seems little likelihood at the moment that gasohol will really take hold.

Similarly, there has been some conversion to LPG as a transportation fuel. Although this helps spread the transportation load a little further across the barrel, it does not, at least so far, really represent an alternative fuel despite its environmental advantages.

Electric cars also have some way to go before becoming a real alternative, despite the advances made in recent years. They will not become commercially viable until problems such as their limited driving range and long stops for recharging have been overcome.

Gas oil, the middle of the barrel, has seen some substitution, but again for non-transportation use. Natural gas has been the main beneficiary of the change. Gas oil's transportation use remains unchallenged and, indeed, is growing with the increasing move to diesel fuel from gasoline. The change has been accelerated in many countries by favourable tax treatment because of perceived environmental advantages: as these come under suspicion the tax treatment may change and gasoline-powered cars may come back into favour.

The main challenge to gasoline has come from increased fuel efficiency, and it is difficult to imagine that car manufacturers will be able to continue the scale of the improvements made in the last twenty years.

This overall pattern of consumption, with increasing demand for the top of the barrel, has led to increasingly severe oil refining, where crude oil is treated at higher temperatures and with a variety of catalysts to convert a higher proportion of the crude to lighter products. This is inevitably more expensive than older methods and has required massive investment from the refining industry.

The refining industry

The proportions of the different products made in a refinery are heavily dependent on the type of crude oil processed. The heavier (literally) crude oils of the Middle East and South America give rise to high volumes of fuel oil but little gasoline, whereas the lighter crude oils of the North Sea, North Africa and the United States produce relatively small amounts of fuel oil, with a low sulphur content which is therefore able to be cracked more easily. (In most modern refineries the heavier products, after straight run refining, are passed on to a secondary cracking process.)

This has made light crudes very much more attractive than heavier ones through most of the last twenty years. This tendency is unlikely to change, for the reasons given earlier, except when occasional external factors, such as suddenly increased electricity demand in non-natural gas areas, alter the balance. The increase in fuel oil cracking has led to some respite for fuel oil, but this is likely to alter again as cracking efficiency increases and technology improves.

Until the early 1960s the major oil companies owned and ran

virtually all of the world's oil refineries, which were largely located in areas convenient to the markets for their products. Thus there are, for example, several refineries in the Amsterdam–Rotterdam–Antwerp (or ARA) area of northern Europe, with its ready access to the Rhine and thence to Germany, Switzerland and the inland areas of Belgium and the Netherlands. Similarly, in the United States there are a number of refineries on the Gulf coast of Texas, where crude oil is produced and imported and access to the inland US markets is easy, though in this case the ease of access has come about more by design.

During the late 1960s and early 1970s the increasing national-isation of crude oil production broke the oil companies' monopoly over the passage of oil from well to consumer. As a result, the oil spot market flourished. With more crude oil available, other companies were able to get involved in refining and this led to the growth of independent refineries. They tended to be built where access to crude oil supply was easy, hence the number of such refineries located on the Italian coast. The independent oil refiners bought crude from the spot markets, processed it and then sold the products back on to the spot market, obviating the need for their own integrated distribution systems.

German legislation, passed in the 1960s to open up the distribution of oil products and reduce the monopoly of the oil majors, also contributed to the growth of independent refining: here was at least one major consumer with an 'open' market. Gradually, independent marketing companies appeared in other countries too, buying oil products from the spot market and retailing them through small distribution systems.

It was the growth of the refining industry on the Italian coast, close to the supply of North and West African crudes, which led to the formation of the secondary European spot market in the Mediterranean. Products dealt in this market are largely consumed by the Mediterranean countries themselves, but when a supply shortage exists in the northern part of the continent the Mediterranean market can be tapped. Similarly, cargoes of gas oil and gasoline are shipped to the United States whenever prices are right.

These independent refineries prospered in the mid 1970s as oil demand grew and prices were steady. Although they had the effect of reducing the profit margin of the majors, there were still profits to be made in oil refining until after the 1979 price boom. The subsequent drop in demand and prices for all oil products made refining un-economic for everybody, large or small, but it put the independent refiners in particular difficulty because they lacked the majors' integrated supply systems and stronger financial position.

More recently, much of the growth has been in the Middle East and Asia Pacific regions. In the case of the former it is largely due to a wish to get added value from crude oil production; in the latter case it is largely for strategic reasons.

Oil refinery economics can be talked about in general terms, though each individual refinery and type of crude oil can generate entirely different figures. In order to run a profitable refinery the selling price of the products must be greater than the combined cost of crude oil, running the refinery, capital depreciation and transportation and distribution costs. Although this seems self-evident there are times when such profits are not made. And the marginal cost of refining, by 'forgetting' capital depreciation and some running costs (such as a labour force which must be paid regardless of the operational capacity), is very much less than the real cost. Thus, whenever the refining of crude oil has been profitable on a marginal cost basis the utilisation of refinery capacity has increased.

The product slates of different crude oils can be varied within a refinery by adjusting the severity of the processing and by upgrading various proportions of the products. With this sort of variability in the mixture of end-products it can be difficult to estimate refinery profitability. But average yields of different crudes are published by oil journals and information services and can be used to give an approximate estimate of profitability. The precise profit of any individual refinery is less important to the trader (within reason) than the trend and by following a consistently calculated estimate some idea of profitability can be obtained.

Refining was generally uneconomic through the first half of the 1980s and was little better in the early 1990s. Refinery closures have been prevented by occasional bouts of real and marginal profitability, usually a result of cold weather or some other short term increase in demand.

Despite the cutbacks, utilisation rates also fell, with Western Europe and the US reaching lows in 1981 of 56 and 68 per cent respectively. Later in the decade utilisation and profitability rose again, led by the gradual increase in demand, and this continued through the 1990s. Table 2.1 gives a breakdown of world oil consumption figures between 1985 and 1996.

Worldwide oil refining capacity is increasing after falls in the early 1990s. The US, Europe and, particularly, Russia have seen declines, although existing capacity is still being upgraded. These falls are more than outweighed, however, by increases in the Middle East and Asia Pacific regions. These last two have seen their share of world refining capacity increase from less than 20 per cent in 1986 to 29.7 per cent ten years later. In the Middle East, for example, refining capacity rose from 3.6 mbd in 1980 to 5.5 mbd in 1996.

Most OPEC countries are becoming increasingly involved in the downstream side of the industry either by building their own refineries, as in the Middle East, or by signing long term supply contracts that involve some transfer of equity with importing nations such as deals done by Mexico and Venezuela.

Table 2.1 World oil consumption (000 barrels/day), 1985-96

	1985	1986	1987	1988	1989	1990
N America	17 900	18 435	18 895	19 590	19 795	19 450
S & C America	3 155	3 315	3 420	3 520	3 570	3 550
Europe	13 880	14 400	14 520	14 705	14 745	14 965
FSU	8 365	8 400	8 440	8 305	8 310	8 405
Middle East	2 995	3 020	3 100	3 085	3 215	3 385
Africa	1 715	1 695	1 765	1 840	1 920	1 975
Asia Pacific	10 465	10 970	11 295	12 160	12 900	13 700
Total world	58 475	60 235	61 435	63 205	64 455	65 430
of which						
OECD %	60.1	60.5	60.2	60.4	60.0	59.5
USA %	25.9	26.0	26.1	26.3	25.9	24.9
EU %	18.0	19.5	19.1	18.9	18.7	18.7

	1991	1992	1993	1994	1995	1996
N. America	19 150	19 430	19 700	20 355	20 175	20 740
S & C America	3 615	3 740	3 825	3 995	4 165	4 335
Europe	14 990	15 005	15 000	15 015	15 300	15 580
FSU	7 995	6960	5570	4 740	4 355	3 935
Middle East	3 480	3540	3645	3 795	3 940	3 960
Africa	2 010	2045	2110	2 160	2 250	2 320
Asia Pacific	14 275	15 255	15 910	17 005	17 910	18 675
Total world	65 515	65 975	65 760	67 065	68 095	69 545
of which						
OECD %	59.5	60.0	60.6	60.9	60.1	60.1
USA %	24.4	24.6	25.0	25.3	24.9	25.0
EU %	19.1	19.3	19.2	18.9	18.8	18.7

N America includes Mexico; EU is European Union.
Source: BP.

The long term effects of these moves will probably take a number of years to make themselves fully felt, but it does seem possible that OPEC could begin to exert more power than it has in the last fifteen to twenty years. Such control will not really be possible until the oil supply balance tilts back in OPEC's favour, probably early in the twenty-first century.

The markets

The history of crude oil outlined in the first chapter cannot be considered on its own in an attempt to understand today's oil markets. During much of the time markets have existed outside the major oil companies, crude oil has been the dominating influence on the price of oil products. The only real exception to that came in the early 1980s when oversupply led to an increasing influence for oil products and it was really the lack of demand for these that led to the sharp fall in prices. Since the end of the 1980s both crude oil and products have had their turn at dominating markets, though crude tends to be more politically sensitive and more attractive to non-oil investors and to attract greater attention as a consequence.

Prior to the 1960s and 1970s, virtually all of the world's oil refining capacity was in the hands of the oil majors. But gradually the independent companies began to set up refineries. Then came the independent refineries, set up for the sole purpose of buying crude on the growing spot market, processing it and selling the products, sometimes on longer term contracts but more usually back on to the spot market. It was these sales that really led to the changes. Whenever refining could be done at a profit these companies stepped in, but whenever refinery economics became too gloomy they withdrew from the market altogether. The majority of these refineries were set up in the Amsterdam–Rotterdam–Antwerp (ARA) area, the Mediterranean coast of Italy, the Gulf of Mexico, the Caribbean and, latterly, Singapore.

These independent refineries were both a natural result of the oil spot markets and a major factor in their development. The spot markets had begun to emerge as more participants appeared in the market and the supply chain from oil well to consumer was no longer in the hands of single entities. They evolved from the need for a balancing mechanism to handle excess supply and demand, and this in turn enabled the independent refineries to use the spot market as a source of supply and a market for products.

Until the early 1980s the oil majors used the spot markets only rarely and admitted they might be useful even less often. But as refining became uneconomic and long term supply contracts were abandoned, the majors were forced to turn to the market more and more. BP, the first of the Seven Sisters wholeheartedly to adopt a trading mentality and the only one to be net short of crude oil at that time, announced in early 1983 that it was buying more than 50 per cent of its crude oil needs from the spot market. Now all oil companies, integrated and otherwise, are extensive users of the spot markets.

Physical markets

The spot crude oil market is a global one. Prices of crude are generally quoted free on board (fob) at their loading port. There is only one market for each crude, with prices the same wherever in the world they are being talked. Most of the traders are based in the areas where there is an active product market, with London, Houston and Singapore having the largest concentrations.

Most crude oil on the physical market is priced as a differential to an actively traded futures or forward market. Instead of buyer and seller agreeing an absolute price for the cargo of crude oil, they agree a floating price. Crude oil is often priced on or around the bill of lading date (when the ship loads the oil): the price is that of the day (or an average of several days) as published by one or more of the price reporting systems or the New York Mercantile Exchange

(NYMEX) or International Petroleum Exchange (IPE) futures contracts. A differential is agreed to reflect differences in quality, timing or other factors between the price basis crude and the actual crude oil dealt. Most oil traded in Europe and many West African crudes, for example, are priced against Brent while almost all crude imported into the US, or traded within it, is priced against NYMEX crude oil futures.

The spot or cash oil product markets are based on five major centres and a number of smaller ones, although the actual trading often takes place many miles from the nominal centre. The five major spot markets today are: north-west Europe, loosely based on the ARA area although the cargo market works primarily out of London; the Mediterranean, based on Italy's west coast but including imports from the Black Sea and through the Suez Canal; the Gulf of Mexico, out of Houston; the Caribbean, including South America; and Singapore, the most recent addition to the list and the fastest growing.

Products are traded more locally. Regional consumption and supply factors mean that prices for individual products vary widely from one area to another. Like crude, products are often traded on a floating price basis around the time the physical transfer of product takes place.

The north-west European market

The north-west European market is the larger of the two in Continental Europe, covering as it does three of the four major European consumers – Germany, the UK and most of France.

Spot market trading in Europe began in the 1950s, when it was a very small and insignificant part of the industry trading very small volumes and being largely ignored by the oil companies, which still had oil marketing their own way. In terms of actual volumes traded the market does not account for even half the oil products used in the region, but its significance far outweighs its size. Virtually all oil sales in the region, including inland sales, are based on the prices established in spot market trading.

The volumes handled are virtually impossible to determine, because a cargo frequently changes hands several times before arriving with an end-user and there are no official records of the trading apart from those held by individual traders. Neither is there any official record of prices: the deals done are generally public knowledge but the information all passes by word of mouth.

There are a number of price reporting systems assessing the deals done on a daily basis and publishing them on screen, fax or telex services. They all rely on using a team of people to telephone around a number of traders to find out what deals have been done and at what price. Although these services have come in for a lot of criticism over the years, the increasing number of them and their resulting competitiveness has improved their accuracy and acceptability. They are used for most traded deals and are the yardstick by which traders' performance is measured.

The price reporting services are also used as a basis for the settlement on the IPE crude oil contract and are being looked at by the IPE and other exchanges for new contracts where problems with physical delivery systems appear otherwise insurmountable.

The former USSR is still a major source of supply for the northwest European gas oil market, though its importance has decreased. Gas oil, including EN590 diesel fuel, accounts for around half of all spot market trading. Gasoline comes from a number of former Soviet Union countries. Oil products generally move more freely round the world than they did a few years ago, with price being the factor determining a cargo of product's destination.

There are many refineries in the region, some operated by the major oil companies and others independently. Independent refineries will operate processing deals whereby traders or others hire refining capacity, bringing in the crude oil and getting it refined in return for payment of a fee. These refineries are also a major source of supply to the market, although much of their production, particularly the majors', goes directly to customers.

Over the past twenty-five years or so several large trading companies have bought refineries, but they have generally become distinctly unattractive assets. Traditionally the independents have been less technologically advanced than the majors. Few traders have made a success of operating refineries, largely because of the large investments needed to make a refinery economically viable. During the 1990s, however, several traders have become financially stronger and have been able to absorb the necessary spending. Whether operating a refinery can become a good investment for them, however, remains to be seen.

Over-capacity in the first half of the 1980s led to drastic cuts in capacity and major upgrading, as discussed in more detail in the previous chapter. Total world capacity then began to return to some sort of balance. In the ten years to 1996 refinery capacity in the Middle East and Asia Pacific regions increased by almost 50 per cent and it now accounts for almost 30 per cent of the world total compared with 22 per cent in the mid 1980s. Product demand growth has been strong in the Asia Pacific, but the growth of refinery capacity in the Middle East has changed supply patterns in other markets.

Interest in refineries has also come from oil producers in the Middle East and South America. Several producer countries have bought in to European and other refining companies, usually giving guaranteed access to crude oil as part of the deal. One of the attractions for the producers is access to the distribution and retail systems of the European companies.

Another important factor in the European market is independent storage. These tanks abound in the ARA area and the exact level of stocks is known to no one but the operator. Most of these independent tanks are rented by the traders. Much of the oil traded on the spot market (and all that delivered on to the IPE) is stored in these tanks. There are similar installations in the other spot market areas, but in the US, for example, demand and production figures for stocks are published weekly, so a closer eye can be kept on changes in demand.

In Europe there have been several attempts to monitor stocks in a similar way to the United States, but they have mostly failed because there is no legal requirement to report. The European Union (EU) has tried on several occasions to institute a monitoring system and although the latest effort has enjoyed more success than most, it has still not become such an institution as the US American Petroleum Institute (API) stocks. There are a number of consultancy firms offering monitoring services with some degree of success.

There are two parts to the north-west European market – barges and cargoes. The barge market trades in 1000–2000 tonne parcels of oil products largely moving down the Rhine into Germany and Switzerland. The term also covers the movement of small quantities of oil into the UK and France. The source of supply for the barge market is primarily the majors' oil refineries on the north-west European coast.

There are a large number of barge traders, many of whom are based in Rotterdam, who trade the barges speculatively as well as moving them from refiner to distributor or direct to end-user.

Although the speculative element of barge trading has declined since the advent of oil futures trading, because of the greater operational difficulties in physical trading, it is still a major part of the industry, resulting in a much larger apparent volume of trade than can be accounted for in barge movements. None the less the overall level of activity is somewhat less than it was fifteen to twenty years ago.

Barges are usually traded on a free on board (fob) basis in the ARA area.

The other major sector of the oil product spot market is the cargo market. Although this is centred in the ARA area, it is a more international market with cargoes frequently moving from one market to another. Each parcel in the cargo markets is normally between 18 000 and 30 000 tonnes, usually priced on a cost insurance freight (cif) basis in north-west Europe, but often on an fob basis elsewhere.

All products are traded on the cargo market, but in Europe gas oil accounts for around half of the market, largely because of the high level of speculative trading. This results in a large part from the fact that the downstream distribution system for gas oil is highly competitive and very much easier to enter than most other retail oil products.

In the United States gasoline is the largest volume product traded, with heating oil (the same product as gas oil) second in line.

The historical basis for the high proportion of gas oil trading in Europe is the independent distribution system for home heating oil (the term gas oil covers both home heating fuel and diesel fuel). Domestic heating oil can be distributed in fairly small volumes and does not require the same infrastructure as, for example, gasoline. In many cases former coal distributors went in to oil when oil began to displace coal as a home heating fuel.

In Germany, legislation was introduced in the 1970s encouraging the setting up of independent marketing companies, in an attempt to reduce the monopoly of the Seven Sisters. These distributors were able to look around for the best source of supply, be it the major oil companies or the independent refiners now putting product on to the growing spot market.

In the mid 1990s a new gas oil specification was introduced: EN590. This is a diesel fuel which varies slightly according to the season. This has split gas oil trading into two distinct parts and followed the rapid growth in the use of diesel cars in Europe. Diesel fuel has to meet slightly different requirements from heating oil.

Another reason that gas oil trading is more active is that gasoline specifications vary widely across Europe, thus constricting the market. This is beginning to change with the Eurograde gasoline specification gaining ever greater currency. This has made the gasoline market more liquid than it was, but the level of activity is still much less than gas oil.

In the United States the situation is very different, with gasoline and heating oil (like gas oil the term is also used to cover diesel fuel) accounting for very similar proportions of the total. This is not only because of the, until recently, country-wide specifications for gasoline but also because gasoline and heating oil account for a similar proportion of total oil demand. Gasoline accounts for around 42 per cent of the US oil product market, whereas in Europe it comes second to middle distillate (gas oil and kerosene) with only 24.5 per cent of the market.

The companies active on the spot market can be divided into two very distinct categories: brokers and traders. Brokers do not take a position on the market; they simply act as an intermediary between buyer and seller, taking payment in the form of a commission. Payment for the oil passes directly from buyer to seller and the broker's involvement ends when the deal is agreed. Brokers are frequently used as a means of keeping the identity of the buyer and seller secret until the deal is arranged – particularly useful when, for example, a major oil company wishes to use the market without word spreading. In the United States they also provide a means of complying with anti-trust legislation for the major oil companies.

The traders, on the other hand, take positions on the market, buying and selling speculatively as well as to meet demand and supply requirements. They expose themselves to large financial risk in the hope of equally large reward. Consequently, it is a precarious life: the 1990s saw several trading companies cease activity or withdraw to concentrate on a specialist market. The oil majors mostly now engage in full-blooded trading activity, not simply buying to meet shortfalls in products and selling surpluses.

Cargoes of Brent blend crude oil are traded on an active forward market with one cargo changing hands many times before any actual delivery is taken. Brent, in addition to being the largest volume crude in the UK North Sea, is the largest volume non-OPEC crude on the international free market (though the US and Russia each produce higher volumes of single crudes) and is a highly speculative market.

Each cargo of 500 000 barrels may be traded many times before it is finally collected from Sullom Voe, the loading terminal for crude from the Brent and other fields. There are around ten to twelve major traders in this market, along with twenty or so smaller ones. The major oil companies and refiners also participate actively in this market. It is not unusual to find one trader or oil company several times in one chain of deals as a cargo moves through thirty or so links. Crude oil is a truly international market and does not fit into any one geographical area.

Trading in a forward market will eventually result in the physical transfer of oil from seller to buyer, but most of the trading done is for hedging purposes. In the case of Brent, the contract requires the seller to give the buyer 15 days' notice of physical lifting dates: hence the forward market is sometimes known as the 15-day market. Once a cargo has been nominated it is known as a dated cargo, with specific loading dates attached to it, and it becomes a normal physical cargo.

Thus from the middle of each month, Brent cargoes become dated and the dated and forward markets co-exist. In mid June, for example, July cargoes will start being nominated. The price of these dated cargoes moves differently from the forward Brent market, reflecting the very short term supply and demand of the crude. In the middle of July the last July cargo is nominated and the prices of dated Brent and July Brent must therefore coincide.

Much of the physical crude traded around the world is priced on dated Brent. This means that the price of, for example, most West African and North Sea crudes will be quoted by traders as 'dated Brent plus x cents' or 'dated Brent minus y cents'. In North and South America many crudes are similarly quoted as a differential to West Texas Intermediate (WTI).

The last ten years have seen the emergence of a new type of trader: the Wall Street refiners. They were given this name when the US investment banks set up oil trading arms to deal in oil derivatives in much the same way as they deal in other financial instruments. They are assuming the risk for a number of companies involved in the oil markets and laying these risks off in the physical or futures markets in the same way as an insurance company does in other sectors. Several of them also take substantial outright positions in their own right. They have been in existence since around 1987 and made an immediate impact on the oil industry worldwide.

The Wall Street refiners' customers come from right across the industry from producers to consumers and they offer more flexibility than the paper or futures markets are usually able to, tailoring options and other instruments to match exactly the customer's requirements. They will then study all the available ways of offsetting the resulting risk and lay it off wherever seems most appropriate. Their charges will normally be built into the cost of the instrument offered.

The Mediterranean market

The smaller of the two European spot markets, the Mediterranean, is supplied primarily by local refineries, particularly the independents situated on the west Italian coast and the islands. There is increasingly important supply from Russia and the former Soviet Union via the Black Sea and this source is likely to become even more significant as oilfields in the region are developed. Oil products from the Arabian Gulf also enter the market.

The Caribbean market

The Caribbean is the smallest of the recognised oil spot markets but it has an important role to play in balancing supply, particularly on the US and European markets. Crude oil is produced and refined in the area, which includes Venezuela, the largest exporter of crude oil to the US, and normally shipped to the US market, though gas oil and fuel oil sometimes find their way to Europe. The market does not trade as actively as its European counterparts.

The Singapore market

The fastest-growing spot market is that in Singapore. It is the youngest of the main spot markets, but has established itself as the centre for trading in south and south-east Asia. This area is primarily served by the developing local refining industry and the Arabian Gulf refiners.

The high demand for light products in the western world has meant that the heavier crude oils produced in the Middle East tend to go east, though increasing production in the region and the slight swing back to heavier crudes forced on the industrial west by the lack of a sufficient supply of sweet crudes has begun to change this.

The Singapore market has flourished, strongly supported by the government. Fuel oil and naphtha have traditionally been the main products traded in the area, naphtha primarily because of Japanese import requirements, though gas oil, jet kero and gasoline are also traded.

Singapore has become the focus of attention for countries as far apart as India and Australia and now enjoys all the infrastructure of the older markets.

The US market

The United States is the second largest crude oil producer in the world with a daily output of some 8.3 million barrels. The remaining 9 million barrels per day (approximately) that it requires are met by imports from all over the world (barring those suppliers banned by the government), but primarily South America, the United Kingdom and Nigeria. The US has traditionally thought of itself as a producing country, but in the last decade it has switched to importing more than it produces domestically as consumption has risen and production declined.

On the Gulf coast and in some other centres, including New York and southern California, there are active spot markets similar to those in Europe, where parcels of product and crude are sold from trader to trader. But the character of the US markets is made different by the pipeline systems which exist to transport crude oil and products around the country. This makes the parcel size very much more flexible than the shiploads traded in Europe (and goes some way towards explaining the runaway success of the NYMEX crude oil futures contract). Elsewhere, for example, crude oil tends to be traded in 400 000 to 500 000 barrel parcels, but in the United States volumes as small as 10 000 barrels may be traded, though larger volumes are more frequent. This has led to a very much more active crude oil spot market, with a much larger number of participants than in Europe, where the financial commitment is so great as to deter all but the largest companies and traders.

Price differentials have existed between Europe and the US for a number of reasons, one of the most important being the cheap domestic crude. Although only Saudi Arabia produces more crude oil, the US government forbids crude oil exports (with some minor exceptions) and the country has never been a major force as a producer in the oil markets. Domestically produced crude has never had to compete on the international market and the price remained unnaturally low, aided by import restrictions on oil products until 1980/81. Since then, the US market has become effectively an international marketplace despite the crude oil export restrictions.

The increasing level of crude imports to the United States has been of concern to the government for some time and whenever crude oil prices have fallen below around $15 per barrel for any length of time the question of an import tax on crude oil is raised. It is unlikely that domestic production can be increased significantly, except in Alaska where environmental issues have long been an important factor in assessing development potential, even before the major oil spill in early 1989.

The futures markets

The oil futures markets were set up to enable traders to offset some of the risks they take; by hedging their positions, or taking a futures position equal and opposite to that which they hold on the physical market. Thus a trader who has bought a cargo of gas oil at a fixed price would sell futures to protect himself against a fall in price before he can sell his cargo.

Commodity futures markets developed in the late eighteenth and early nineteenth centuries as trade grew first nationally and then internationally. They developed from the corn exchanges seen in almost every town of any size, where merchants, producers and consumers used to gather to trade. As the time lag between growth and actual sale grew, because of the distances covered in the transit of products, it became necessary to hold stocks and anticipate future supply and demand. Markets began to be affected by non-local factors and prices became more erratic. These developments were particularly noticeable in international commodities such as cotton, sugar, coffee and cocoa where there were several weeks or months between harvest and sale.

Many people date futures trading from the American Civil War when English cotton mills bought American cotton before it had been shipped; though there is some evidence that futures trading existed in some ancient civilisations.

Although the origins of modern futures trading were in England, the largest commodity trading centre is now Chicago, where there are two large commodity exchanges trading contracts in a wide range of agricultural products, financial instruments and metals. Contracts range from orange juice, meat products and grains through precious and other metals to foreign currencies, bonds and stock market indices.

There has been rapid growth in futures trading since the mid 1970s, with a large number of contracts opening up, particularly in America. Many of these contracts, like the energy futures in Chicago, the first fuel oil in New York and the first two crude oils in London, never really get off the ground, but a large number do become successful, with some of the financial instruments in Chicago regularly recording the trade of more than 250 000 contracts in a single day.

It took several years for oil futures trading to become fully integrated with the oil industry. But the usefulness of the futures themselves and the instruments that have developed around them has overcome the initial scepticism of the trade and changed the way in which it operates.

As the oil markets generally become increasingly international and the reporting systems disseminate information instantly, the opportunities for older trading techniques have diminished and new methods are having to be found. Futures trading has opened up a number of new possibilities, many of which are being used increasingly by an industry used to adapting itself quickly to outside changes. Perhaps the most useful function the markets can perform long term is the separation of price and supply, and it is this that led to the real integration of futures. For example, a large proportion of gas oil traded in Europe changes hands on an EFP basis (see Chapter 6).

The futures contracts

In 1997 there were seven successful energy contracts, five of them in oil, and three newly introduced contracts whose success is as yet uncertain. The most successful is the New York Mercantile Exchange's (NYMEX) West Texas Intermediate crude oil contract, which averages around 100 000 contracts (100 million barrels) per day and has traded in excess of 225 000 contracts in a day. All the oil contracts have seen year on year growth virtually every year since their introduction.

The NYMEX also operates two other contracts – heating oil and unleaded gasoline. Heating oil was the first successful oil futures contract, introduced in November 1978. The other established and successful futures contracts traded are natural gas in New York and Brent crude, natural gas and gas oil on London's International Petroleum Exchange (IPE). Options are traded on all these contracts except the IPE's natural gas. There is also a propane contract on NYMEX which has traded for many years but has a generally low volume. There are also contracts in fuel oil in Singapore and electricity on NYMEX which have yet to establish themselves, though at least one of the electricity contracts is likely to succeed.

Propane

The propane contract is the oldest currently trading, although it has transferred from the New York Cotton Exchange where it started life in 1971 to the NYMEX. It is not a successful contract, despite its longevity, and still trades only a few contracts a day.

Between its inception and the opening of the heating oil contract in 1978 there were a number of attempts to introduce energy futures trading elsewhere, in both Europe and the United States. There were two reasons why these were unsuccessful: first, and most importantly, was that the time was wrong; secondly, the siting of the markets was wrong. Timing is essential for all new futures markets. Futures markets depend on volatility in prices and the 1970s saw, more or less, a steady rise in prices, at least until the Iranian revolution. Even the heating oil contract had a very quiet start because prices were effectively moving in one direction.

The siting of markets in major financial centres was also important because all futures markets require a financial infrastructure to support the clearing mechanism. This was missing from most of the early attempts at introducing new contracts.

NYMEX No. 2 heating oil contract

In 1978 the NYMEX introduced its No. 2 heating oil contract and a No. 6 fuel oil contract. Interest from both the oil industry and the essential speculative element of the market was slow to develop initially and the fuel oil contract failed to progress. After a time trading stopped altogether. Heating oil, on the other hand, very slowly began to attract interest and the violent price rises of 1979 and 1980 enabled the market to establish itself.

As a product, heating oil satisfied the major criteria necessary for an active contract – it was heavily traded on the free market, relatively easy to specify, store and transport and, as a result, to deliver. Although physical delivery is not, and should not be, the main function of a futures market, every contract must be supported by a sound, realistic delivery procedure to gain the confidence of the industry and to ensure a close price correlation between the 'paper' futures contract and the 'wet' physical oil market. Nevertheless, in its first year or so, the heating oil contract failed to capture the imagination of the oil industry in New York and the US coast of the Gulf of Mexico. The market traded very low volumes, sometimes only one or two contracts per day, and was not making the progress that had been hoped for. Gradually, however, the exchange's marketing and education programme, at the time the most ambitious and deliberate campaign ever mounted by a commodity exchange, began to bear fruit. Interest in the market began to increase and, as the traders tested the market, liquidity began to improve and reach sustainable levels, attracting still more interest. By the mid 1990s the market was regularly trading 35 000 lots per day and on occasion has reached more than 100 000 lots. The open interest averages around the 120 000 mark. (Open interest, which represents the number of lots which remain uncovered on any day and would therefore have to be delivered if the market were to cease trading, is often taken as a better guide to the liquidity of a market than its daily turnover.)

The slow start was inevitable in retrospect. The oil industry was positively antagonistic to the concept of futures trading, entirely new to almost everyone in the trade. This antagonism was to be repeated in Europe a few years later when the London market opened. The list of advantages attached to futures trading is usually headed by the opportunity of hedging, the laying off of risk and locking in a profit in case the market turns against you. This idea was anathema to an industry which had made vast sums of money by taking on the risks it was now being asked to avoid.

Probably the main reason for the collective change of mind was the two-directional volatility seen in oil prices after 1980. Before then, oil prices had only ever been stable or moved sharply upwards – weakening levels were almost always short-lived and slight. But the last twenty years or so has seen oil become a true commodity market, with two-way price volatility.

IPE gas oil contract

After the New York heating oil contract, the next to be introduced was the International Petroleum Exchange's gas oil contract in

London. Gas oil is the European name for heating oil and, although there are some specification differences between the two contracts, the product is essentially the same. When the contract was introduced, in April 1981, the IPE began a similar, though smaller scale, marketing campaign to that carried out by NYMEX three years earlier. A small proportion of the European industry had used the heating oil contract, but essentially the IPE faced the same problems NYMEX had had. US import controls had meant that there was not necessarily any correlation between US and European prices, so the traders who had tried out the New York market had tended to treat it as a bit of a game.

The London gas oil contract had a steady start with volumes gradually increasing to their current levels: in 1997 gas oil traded an average of around 16 000 contracts/day.

Like the NYMEX in New York, the IPE adopted an active marketing policy. It was the first London commodity market to do this and the idea was treated somewhat sceptically by its soft commodity and metals equivalents. The success of the approach won over the other markets, however, and the idea was adopted more aggressively, and even more successfully, by the London International Financial Futures Exchange a few months later.

NYMEX leaded gasoline contract

Having established a solid trading base, both exchanges were well placed to introduce further contracts. The NYMEX was the first to take the plunge, introducing a leaded regular gasoline contract in late 1982. The contract was reasonably successful, growing quite well although it remained less active than heating oil until it ceased trading (having been replaced with an unleaded gasoline contract) in 1986. The unleaded gasoline contract is fully established and averages a volume of around 30 000 contracts/day. It endured difficult trading conditions during the mid 1990s as a result of various legislative changes to gasoline introduced for environmental reasons. By late 1996, however, most of these had been resolved and gasoline trading recovered.

NYMEX crude oil contract

Six months after the original gasoline contract was introduced, four new markets were opened, one on the NYMEX and three in Chicago. New York opened a crude oil contract, based on West Texas Intermediate (WTI), and the Chicago Board of Trade (CBT) brought in heating oil, unleaded regular gasoline and crude oil, based on Light Louisiana Sweet. Of these, only the NYMEX crude contract had any degree of success and the three contracts in Chicago soon stopped trading.

The New York crude oil contract quickly became the most successful oil futures contract ever introduced (if you use open interest as the measure of success), attracting enormous interest from trade and speculator alike and rapidly becoming a focal point for the entire oil industry, even those not actually using the exchange. The success of the contract did not dispel criticism from some parts of the industry, but the volume of trade and the quality of the participants soon made it impossible to ignore, even for the most die-hard industry conservatives. It was largely this contract that led to the complete integration of futures trading with traditional industry practice and the rapid development of other risk management instruments.

Within eighteen months all but two of the original Seven Sisters (now Six Sisters, since the Chevron and Gulf merger) were using the exchange to some extent, and its influence was to be felt throughout the world. Virtually all US and European oil refiners and traders now use the exchange, and Asian and Australasian traders, too, are becoming increasingly involved.

Although still based on WTI, the contract is now known as a light sweet crude contract. Various other crude grades specified by NYMEX can be delivered against the contract with exchange set differentials applied.

The 'exchange for physicals' method of delivery, whereby a long and a short can mutually agree to deliver any crude at any place, with a differential price against WTI if necessary, gave a major boost to the contract. Almost all the deliveries against the crude oil futures contract are made using this procedure.

IPE crude oil contract

The next energy contract to be introduced was the International Petroleum Exchange's first crude oil contract, based on the primary North Sea crude, Brent Blend. This started trading in November 1983 but quickly faded into obscurity.

One major problem faced by the IPE in introducing a crude oil contract was delivery. Under the rules of trading it must be possible to deliver one lot of a commodity traded on the futures market. In the United States, with its pipeline systems and major terminals such as Cushing, Oklahoma (chosen by New York) and St James, Louisiana the delivery procedure could be fairly simple. It is possible to deliver relatively small (5000 barrels) quantities of crude oil. In the United States anyone delivering less than five lots of crude oil must do so in a tank storage installation. But in Europe even 5000 barrels is too small for an oil terminal to handle. The whole system is geared to quantities of 400 000 barrels upwards.

Thus, the IPE contract wilted. But the European crude oil trade, although using the NYMEX contract actively, none the less felt the need for a crude futures contract more closely allied to their own business and pressure was exerted on the IPE to find some way of developing a new Brent futures contract as soon as possible. This pressure was increased during the winter of 1984/85 when the differential between WTI and Brent moved more than the absolute price of crude oil, making WTI unacceptable as a hedging vehicle to most traders.

A number of ways of developing a new market were studied. The most attractive was the establishing of a crude oil price index, based on published price data for spot deals on the Brent market, which could then be used as a basis for cash settlement. Thus, when a delivery month expires, and delivery would normally take place, physical oil does not change hands but the current market value of the oil does, enabling buyer and seller to achieve the same financial position they would have been in with the oil. Such an index was introduced in May 1985.

The oil industry's reaction was cautiously approving and a contract based on cash settlement began trading in November 1985. When a contract expired, all outstanding positions were settled in cash at the average of the preceding five days' indices. Again this had a somewhat cautious welcome from the trade and the market gradually faded away again.

But the pressure from the industry continued and a third attempt was made by the IPE in 1988 with the introduction of a Brent contract settled in cash but using the index for one day only rather than the five-day average used previously. This contract was successful from the start, receiving great support from the industry and the brokerage community. Volume and open interest grew steadily, with the contract averaging more than 42 000 contracts a day by the mid 1990s.

The concept of cash settlement was readily accepted by the oil industry. It is particularly useful where physical delivery provisions are impossible or awkward. Several contracts currently under consideration by the exchanges are likely to use cash settlement. The main requirement for a cash settlement contract is an accurate and reliable means of establishing a settlement price: Brent uses all the available published sources. The concept of cash settlement may lead to a further development: a futures contract based on, for example, a basket of crudes. Many crude oils, particularly in the Asia Pacific region, are priced against a number of other crudes: these could be combined into an index.

Brent crude is traded on SIMEX during the Singapore working day under a reciprocal arrangement with the IPE. It has not been a success, attracting very little interest and trading only slowly.

SIMEX fuel oil market

In February 1989 the Singapore International Monetary Exchange (SIMEX) introduced its first oil futures contract, for high sulphur fuel oil. This had a reasonably good start but failed to develop. The contract attracted a high degree of interest before it opened because it was the first oil contract to be opened in the Far East but this was not enough to ensure its success. The contract was eventually withdrawn. It was reintroduced some years later but again failed.

Natural gas

Both NYMEX and the IPE have introduced natural gas contracts in recent years. The US exchange, indeed, has introduced several. The first, and most successful, has been the Henry Hub contract. Henry Hub is a major pipeline distribution centre in Louisiana. Further contracts based on other centres have been less successful.

One of the problems with natural gas, and electricity, is that the physical markets are less developed than oil and the delivery systems and centres are not as well established. One approach is to introduce more than one contract and let some fail while others succeed as the physical trading systems develop.

The Henry Hub gas contract, introduced in 1990, exceeded even light sweet crude in its early growth and by 1997 was trading around 47 000 contracts per day.

The IPE introduced its natural gas contract in early 1997, as soon as the deregulated gas balancing system in the UK had achieved a successful cycle. The contract has had a good start, attracting a great deal of interest. It is likely to see real growth when the Interconnector, a pipeline enabling gas to move between the UK and Continental Europe, is opened in 1998.

The gas transmission system in the UK enables a simple delivery procedure to be used by the IPE and the contract has seen very high levels of delivery in its first few months.

The natural gas contract is the first one introduced by the main energy exchanges to be traded exclusively electronically. Traders can either put their orders through a broker, in the normal way, or they can become members of the market, using an exclusive gas membership, and use their own screens.

Options

There are now traded options on all the NYMEX and IPE futures contracts except the IPE natural gas contracts. The option contracts have attracted some interest, but energy options have generally traded a lower proportion of the underlying futures volume than most other commodities. This is due in large part to the high volatility seen in oil prices: volatility is often in the 25–35 per cent range, compared with 10–15 per cent on many other commodities. This leads to high, and hence unattractive to many, premiums and makes options an expensive way of dealing with risk when compared with many others.

Despite the difficulties, WTI options trade around 22 000 contracts per day with gasoline and heating oil on NYMEX trading around 5000 contracts each. Brent options average around 1500 lots per day and gas oil a few hundred. Exchange options have been seriously affected by the growth of average price options on the over-the-counter market. The exchanges are looking at ways of introducing such options.

The paper refinery

The introduction of crude oil futures opened up the way to the crack spread or paper refinery. All oil refiners operate on the margin between the cost of crude oil and the value of products produced, but when the crude oil is purchased the exact selling price of the products cannot be determined. Using the futures markets, however, refinery margins can be traded on paper. At the point where the premium of the value of products over the cost of crude makes refining economic, the product contracts are sold and the crude bought on the assumption that refinery runs will increase and the margin decline. When this happens, the crude is sold and the products bought back. If refining is far from economic, the reverse can be done, because refinery runs will fall until the margin widens.

This spread, known as the crack spread, involves having an equal number of product contracts (split roughly 2:1 or 3:2 gasoline to heating oil) to crude contracts on NYMEX or 4:3 gas oil to crude on the IPE.

The split reflects the yield of a standard refinery, but of necessity omits the heavier end of the barrel. No successful fuel oil contract has yet been introduced, but fuel oil (or, indeed, the whole refinery margin) can be dealt with on the swaps market (see Chapter 8).

Possible new contracts

All exchanges are constantly looking at possible new futures contracts. In the US all new contracts have to be approved by the Commodities Futures Trading Commission, the US regulatory body, while on the IPE this approval must be given by the Financial Services Authority (formerly the Securities and Investments Board).

In the immediate future, NYMEX is proposing to introduce a coal futures contract during the latter part of 1998 and a sour crude contract, whilst the IPE is looking at various contracts including electricity and several oil products including jet fuel.

Sour crude and fuel oil are perhaps the two biggest missing market sectors. Both the IPE and NYMEX have had sour crude oil contracts in the past, but neither have been successful. Differentials between Brent and WTI and sour crudes can be very volatile, making the hedging of sour crude on existing futures contracts difficult.

Both exchanges have had similar difficulties with fuel oil contracts and these too may be tried again. The IPE may also consider gasoline again: previously the large number of gasoline grades traded in Europe have made a gasoline contract difficult, but the increasing use of Eurograde gasoline could make a contract possible.

From the other side of the fence, the industry has now grown so accustomed to futures contracts that it now lobbies the exchanges for the contracts it would like to have. A heavy crude oil contract and fuel oil probably have the strongest supporters, but there are also demands for futures markets in jet fuel, naphtha and other small volume products. It is unlikely that a futures market in either jet fuel or naphtha would succeed in Europe or the United States, in the case of jet fuel because of the unusual nature of the market and naphtha because of the small number of participants. Naphtha might possibly succeed in the Far East, in either Singapore or Tokyo, because of the active market based around Japanese import requirements. It remains to be seen how well the new contracts succeed.

The demands for heavy fuel oil and heavy crude both stem from the increasing amount of cracking and the relative recovery in demand for heavy fuel oil. One problem encountered in establishing a fuel oil contract is that the fuel oil market is divided roughly into two parts: utilities and ship's bunker fuel. The former includes demand from power stations and industry. There are some significant specification differences between the two and the IPE's failure with its first fuel oil contract was largely due to compromise, introducing elements from both specifications to produce a hybrid contract for a product which did not exist.

The introduction of new futures contracts is now strongly influenced by the over-the-counter market. Swaps, which are similar to over-the-counter futures contracts, can be introduced more quickly than futures contracts because they do not need regulatory approval. And although a liquid market is necessary for swaps, it is not necessary to have such a high level and swap markets continue in conditions in which futures might not.

There is a strong argument to be made that most oil products and some crude contracts would benefit from having a trading vehicle available to provide active open outcry or electronic trading virtually twenty-four hours a day. Ideally such contracts should be offset against each other, but rivalry between exchanges means that normally each one wants to introduce its own.

Both the IPE and NYMEX have had a number of failed contracts over the years: the problems with Brent were described earlier, but the IPE has also had difficulties with naphtha, gasoline and fuel oil while NYMEX has been unsuccessful with heating oil and gasoline with Gulf coast delivery, sour crude and two of the natural gas contracts.

Electronic trading

The IPE's natural gas contract was the first energy contract to be traded only electronically, but NYMEX introduced electronic trading to the energy markets in the early 1990s. All NYMEX contracts can be traded in the hours between the market's closure and its reopening the following morning (including Sunday night) using the NYMEX Access® system. This simulates open outcry trading, with bids and offers matched on the screen. Volumes vary, but the system has proved useful on occasions where there has been a significant price change during the New York night. NYMEX is now planning to develop the system further.

Automated trading systems can be used to trade smaller contracts where the volume of business is insufficient to sustain the infrastructure needed for an open outcry market. It might be possible, for example, to have a naphtha contract operated in this way.

There seems little doubt, however, that screen trading systems will be developed further over the next few years. If they are as effective as the existing open outcry market, and more particularly if they are cheaper, they will attract a considerable amount of business. If not, after a trial period participants will want to return to the open outcry market. Some combination of the two systems seems likely to provide the way forward for the futures markets.

The future

Futures trading is now an integral part of the oil industry and its future seems assured, whether on screens or an open outcry trading floor. The nature of the industry has changed over the last few years with the growth of the over-the-counter market. Much futures business is now done by the providers of the over-the-counter instruments, who use futures to offset their risk.

More futures contracts are, however, likely to be introduced, particularly if some smaller contracts are traded electronically.

At present, both of the large energy futures exchanges, NYMEX and the IPE, are membership organisations: members receive trading rights and run the exchange, through an executive. Some newer exchanges, in other fields, have been set up as private companies and in late 1997 the IPE began looking at the possibility of becoming a private company.

5

Entering the futures market

The decision to trade

There are almost as many ways for the oil industry to use the futures market as there are users. Just as no two physical trading companies operate in an identical way, so too will their futures market usage vary. But most will find some occasions on which futures trading is an invaluable tool to help in limiting the risks involved in the physical market.

The decision to use futures should only be taken after careful consideration of the various methods of trading and of the operation of the markets themselves. Although the physical and futures markets move closely together, they are, on occasion, subject to different influences and prices will diverge in the short term, though they must realign in any market with a realistic delivery process. Figure 5.1 illustrates this on the NYMEX heating oil futures and New York Harbor heating oil barge market.

Physical business can be enhanced by futures trading in a number of ways. The straight hedge allows a trader to get protection for an unattractive physical position, or a distributor can buy futures ahead and then offer a fixed price to his customers based on that price.

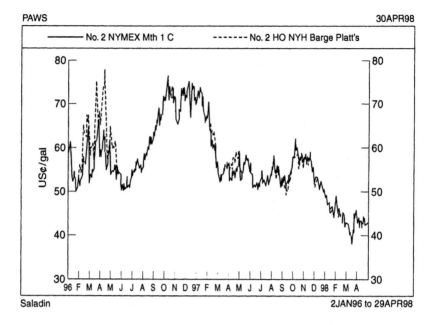

5.1 Heating oil price 1997/98 (source: Saladin).

To date, consumers have been less interested in futures markets than other sectors of the oil industry. This is partly because many consumers feel they are not in the business of anticipating oil prices and just have to pay whatever the market is at the time. In some areas, notably airlines, this has changed. The development of the swaps market has encouraged the participation of more consumers. There are two main reasons for this. Swaps are particularly attractive for those who are unable or unwilling to use futures markets, whether because of company reasons, exchange rate difficulties or whatever: many consumers are in this category. Secondly, swaps are unwound at the monthly average price for the product. This is the pricing mechanism used by many large consumers and therefore reduces basis risk. Average prices can be created on the futures market by lifting the hedge pro rata through the month, but many companies prefer the swap as straightforward hedge.

In New York and London the use of the EFP (exchange for physicals), whereby a futures position is exchanged for a physical one, is widespread and accounts for most of the deliveries in any month. It is now possible to do this on all the oil futures markets, both crude and products. Details of the EFP are given on page 71.

One of the main attractions of EFPs is that they enable both sides to choose any time between the deal being agreed and delivery taking place (or sometimes even later) to price the contract. The danger of being caught by a temporary movement in prices is therefore considerably lower than in a normal Platt's-related or similar deal based on the price on one particular day, or a range of days. A large number of spot market deals are based on the prices reported by one of the telex price services, particularly Platt's. A deal is struck with the price defined as a relationship to the published price on, for example, bill of lading day.

The liquidity of the futures market makes it very much easier to trade than physicals if, for example, a supply department is uncertain whether its refinery will produce enough product to meet commitments. Say, for example, the supply department suspects it may be short of a cargo, but will not be certain for a few more days. In the meantime, it fears that prices may rise, so it buys futures. Then, when the shortfall is confirmed the physical cargo can be bought and the futures sold, but the lower price will be ensured. On the other hand, if there is no shortage, the futures can simply be sold out.

At other times a company may have excess stock, which is costing money to store and finance. When prices are suitable, it is sometimes possible to 'lend' product to a futures market. In this case, product is delivered on to the market one month and taken off the next month, thus freeing up capital and storage space for the intervening period. In practice this is uncommon in oil markets because quality considerations usually outweigh the financial benefit.

With the advent of a wider range of crude oil and products markets, there are also possibilities of trading the refinery margin, the so-called 'paper refinery' (see pages 47 and 68), particularly in New York where the gasoline and heating oil contracts allow for a fairly full coverage of the barrel.

The tendency of the futures market to react short term to events and influences of little or no interest to the oil industry is no reason not to use the market, but it should be understood that the two markets, futures and physical, are different. Any divergence should be treated as an additional trading opportunity. The futures markets are often criticised by the oil industry for failing to react, or overreacting, to certain influences, but, although there is a speculative element in the market, the vast majority of trading is done by the oil industry itself. Studies on the NYMEX suggest that the oil industry accounts on average for about 85 per cent of trading, with the speculative element proportionately lower on the busiest days. In London the trade element is probably over 90 per cent. So although the locals, commodity funds and other speculators may distort the market for a while, they cannot control it indefinitely.

Similarly, the use of price charts to make trading decisions, known as technical trading (see Chapter 10), often dismissed by physical oil traders, can be a strong short-term influence on the markets and should not therefore be ignored. Neither, however, should it be taken as a reason not to trade the markets. All markets with a sound delivery process, be it cash settlement or a conventional physical delivery, must stay in line with their cash products in the long term. So, rather than ignore short term influences, the physical oil trader should seek to take advantage of them.

Choosing a broker

Once a trader has decided to enter the market, the next step is to choose a broker, Each market floor has a finite number of members, and all business must be conducted through these members. In London most of the futures brokers active in the oil market have floor membership, but in New York there are a number of brokers who operate entirely from the floor but cannot clear and others with clearing but no floor operations as well as those with more orthodox floor and office operations.

The choice of broker to use is a personal one, often coming down to the relationship between the individuals in the companies concerned, but there are some guidelines to use. For example, a large company trading high volumes will probably want to choose two or three brokers used to handling large orders. A smaller user may prefer a smaller broker, who will have more time to discuss the market but may charge higher commissions. Different brokers specialise in different areas of the business: there are some on both the IPE and NYMEX who specialise in serving the oil industry and others who offer a broader investment programme for the individual speculator. In New York many of the floor members are 'locals' whose main business is to trade, moving in and out of the market several times a day for their own account. They can be very influential short term on the price movements, but help to provide liquidity on the market. Locals on NYMEX can also execute client orders on the floor. These have to be given up to a clearing member at the end of the day. There are a few locals on the IPE. They can execute orders for other brokers but are not allowed to deal directly with clients.

A company choosing two or more brokers may well decide to choose one specialising in the industry and another with good technical information in order to provide a wider view. Having too many brokers is likely to lead to confusion, but using more than one not only allows for a different opinion but prevents any one broker, however trustworthy, having a complete picture of a trader's position – a factor considered important by many companies. It is also possible, and increasingly common, to execute orders through several brokers but clear through just one.

Another factor considered by some companies is the way the futures broker pays its employees. Some pay their dealers a basic salary plus a profit-related bonus while others pay the dealer a proportion of all commissions generated. There are arguments to be made for each case, but it is useful to know which system is operating for the brokers being used.

The rules and regulations covering futures trading (apart from the market rules) are somewhat different in the United States, the United Kingdom and elsewhere. In the United States, the Commodities Futures Trading Commission (CFTC) is the government agency concerned with futures trading and all brokerage activities are subject to its rules. All brokers are also members of the National Futures Association (NFA), the self-governing regulatory body which deals with futures broking. The NFA is financed by a levy paid on each futures contract traded on a US exchange.

In the United Kingdom, the Financial Services Authority (FSA) is the regulatory body for both commodity markets and brokers. Like its US counterparts it has responsibility for monitoring exchanges, including the approval of new contracts, and can impose penalties on both exchanges and brokers if they break the rules.

Elsewhere regulation is being developed, usually along the lines of the US or UK legislation. In general, regulations imposed in any country govern all business carried out on exchanges in that country or by brokers working in that country. Although regulation differs from place to place, the general principles are more or less the same: to ensure good financial and trading practice within futures brokers and exchanges and consequently a high level of service to customers.

One of the main differences between the US and UK legislation is that US brokers are not allowed to give credit to their customers, while UK brokers are. There are controls and monitors imposed by the FSA on the amount of credit that can be granted: these are designed to ensure that no UK broker becomes so exposed to one customer that the customer's failure to perform can force the broker out of business or prevent its fulfilling its obligations to other clients. In practice US brokers can normally make arrangements through related companies: most brokers are part of large banks or other substantial organisations.

Another difference is that US brokers are obliged to keep all client monies in separate bank accounts from the broker's own funds. In the United Kingdom, the client is able to choose whether it wants its funds segregated from the broker's or not. This may affect commission rates and financing charges.

Clearing

Every futures exchange has a clearing mechanism which guarantees all the trades on the market, once they have been correctly registered. The clearing house registers all trades made on the exchange floor, allocates them to the members and effectively steps in as buyer to every seller and seller to every buyer. A trade is executed on the floor between two brokers but as soon as it is registered with the clearing house it becomes two separate positions held with the clearing house. In this way, when a closing trade is made, the position with the clearing house can simply be closed without reference to any other broker's position.

All exchanges have clearing members, who are authorised to hold positions on that market with the relevant clearing house. These members are not necessarily futures brokers, but may be large users of the market. They are not necessarily present on the floor of the market, and neither are all floor brokers necessarily clearing members.

All trades on a market must be executed through a floor broker. These are the brokers actually on the floor of the market authorised by the exchange to trade. Most floor members are also clearing members and so can hold their clients', and if applicable their own, positions. Others are not and have to 'give up' all trades to a clearing member. They are paid a fee for their floor execution.

Clearing members are responsible to the clearing house for the trades registered in their name. Unlike physical brokers, futures brokers are the principal to the market. This enables clients to maintain anonymity, but means that care should be taken to check the financial viability of the futures broker before opening a trading relationship. Some large users of the market prefer to become clearing members themselves. Although they then have to pay membership fees and subscriptions, and on some markets buy seats on the floor, they usually enjoy lower clearing fees and also have the facility to trade with a number of brokers but have only one overall position. Their exposure is then to the clearing house rather than to any individual broker.

The clearing houses differ from market to market. The IPE is cleared by the London Clearing House (LCH), an organisation owned by the major UK brokers and exchanges. Both SIMEX and NYMEX are cleared by what are effectively mutual corporations of their members, supported by the financial resources of those members. In all cases the guarantees are virtually identical. All clearing houses are financed by a fee payable on each lot traded.

In order to provide the financial guarantee, the clearing house charges an initial margin or deposit on each lot held overnight. These initial margins are set by the exchange/clearing house and can be varied at any time if the clearing house believes market conditions warrant either an increase or a decrease. These are normally around $750 per lot on the IPE and $1000 per lot on NYMEX. They can be varied for individual members or, more normally, for the market as a whole. Initial margins can be paid in the form of T-bills or some other security. If paid by cash, interest is paid by the clearing house.

Each day, all futures positions are margined in full by the clearing house using a process called marking to market. All futures positions are revalued on a daily basis at the previous night's settlement price. Any loss is paid to the clearing house and any profit paid to the clearing member. Thus if a crude oil contract is bought for $20/bbl and the market closes at $19.90 the clearing house will revalue the position at $19.90 and receive 10c/bbl from the clearing member, who will in turn receive it from their client. If the market settles the following day at $20.10 the position is revalued again and the clearing member will be paid 20 c/bbl; again this will be passed on to the client. The amount of this difference is called the variation margin and has to be paid in cash.

Futures commissions

Another cost of trading is the commission payable to futures brokers for business transacted. The level of the commission has to be negotiated and will depend on the volume of business being done and the service required from the broker. For example, some clients like to choose their own floor brokers while others execute and clear through the same broker.

Futures commissions differ from physical market brokerage in that the futures broker has to pay market fees and clearing fees for each lot traded and does not therefore retain the full amount. Some brokers quote their charges inclusive of fees; others break them down. It should also be remembered that the broker is the principal to the market and is therefore assuming market risk whenever it trades for a client. Most companies will make some arrangement with their broker covering minimum cash movements and similar administrative arrangements. Clearing members cannot make such arrangements with the clearing house.

In the United States, futures brokers are required to submit a report to the CFTC each day showing all positions of more than 25 lots in any one month held by their clients. On the IPE the client's identity is known only to the broker until the exchange starts to monitor positions in the run up to expiry.

NYMEX also imposes restrictions on the total position any one client can hold on the market. Some of these restrictions can be eased upon application from the client to NYMEX, which requires evidence that a company needs to hold large futures positions to hedge its physical positions. Clearing members too have their overall position limited by the amount of money (excluding margins) held with the clearing house under its mutual structure.

An oil company trading on the markets will initially find it helpful to discuss with its broker what its purpose is in trading in futures. It is not necessary to give too many details, but a general outline will enable the broker to give better advice. It must be remembered that, unlike the physical market, there is great secrecy surrounding futures activity. No broker divulges the names or trading positions of a client, so the client will not suffer from telling the broker whether a proposed trade is a hedge, a speculative trade or whatever. Although brokers will not be able or even wish to change a client's mind about the position, they will be able to give advice on timing, the state of the market at any given time (for example, it can be almost impossible to trade large volumes during quiet periods) and likely short term developments.

A technical trader, who bases a trading system on various charting methods, will not look for any advice from the broker – indeed a true chartist should take no notice whatsoever of any fundamental information that may be offered.

In London and New York the oil futures markets are used to an unusual degree by the oil industry itself, as opposed to general investors and speculators. Recent studies in New York suggest that the oil industry accounts for 85 per cent of the activity in crude oil, while London estimates trade participation at 90 per cent. The crude oil market attracts more non-trade business than the products market because of the intrinsic appeal of crude oil, like gold, to the speculator.

Despite this high level of trade involvement, the markets have technically behaved 'well', encouraging the commodity funds to come into the market. The oil trade sometimes worries about the activity of speculative traders in 'its' market, but it must be remembered that the speculators help to take on the risk the oil industry is trying to lay off and also improve liquidity.

Several large funds are now involved in the oil markets. They tend to enter the market periodically in very large volume. Some then maintain these positions for several months, rolling them forward as months expire. Others are more sensitive to short term changes and alter positions more frequently. Generally, the funds' influence on the market is short-lived.

In-house administration

Almost as important as the choice of broker is the setting up of effective in-house administration systems. Several European and US oil traders have suffered from having their futures operations physically separate from their spot market activities. Although it may be necessary for different individuals to take responsibility, it is not practicable to run a futures book separately from a physical book as effective use of the futures market necessitates a close interaction between the two.

Many trading desks now have a nominated futures executor. And with larger companies this individual may operate as an in-house clearer, executing trades for several companies within a group. This prevents one person or subsidiary buying while another is selling: the in-house broker can assign purchases to one and sales to another without going into the market. When one side wants to close the position the executor can go to the market to make the trade so that the required position is maintained. Prices can then be allocated in-house. This can result in a significant reduction in trading costs: not only is brokerage reduced but also execution risk.

The mechanics of futures trading

Although exchange practices and regulations vary from market to market, there is one thing that all futures markets have in common. This is the conduct of trading, except of EFPs, by open outcry between a restricted number of members on a trading floor between certain hours. In London all floor members are companies, required by IPE regulations to meet certain capital and other financial criteria, but in the United States memberships are held by individuals and used either by their companies or by the individuals themselves. These individuals are known as 'locals' and trade primarily on their own behalf, moving in and out of the market several times a day and helping to provide liquidity. They also execute client orders.

London does have a local category of membership, but it is small. The IPE's locals may not execute client orders directly.

Open outcry

Under the open outcry system, bids and offers are shouted across the floor of the market until agreement is reached. The two dealers concerned then agree the number of lots traded and the deal is registered and reported back to the client. This reflects the origins of futures markets in corn exchanges and similar open markets. Although it has traditionally been used in trading pits on the market floor it is increasingly being simulated in screen trading systems.

NYMEX contracts are traded electronically during most of the time the market floor is closed, creating a virtually 24-hour market. The IPE's natural gas contract became the first energy contract to be introduced entirely electronically. Both the ACCESS® system and the IPE's simulate open outcry: traders can also get an idea about the depth of the market, i.e. the buyers and sellers behind the current best bids and offers and the size available.

In late 1997 the IPE and NYMEX announced that they were going to develop jointly a new electronic trading system for all energy contracts. Electronic systems seem likely to increase in the future: they offer a much cheaper alternative to floor operations making lower volume contracts feasible. It is also possible to offer longer trading hours. It remains to be seen whether electronic trading will supersede floor trading or complement it.

Orders

Mechanically, futures trading is simple to operate. There are several ways of giving an order to a broker, but in all cases the order is executed on the floor of the market and then registered and cleared in the normal way. The means of confirming an order to the client vary a little but are normally determined by the client. Market practice is normally verbal confirmation, followed at the end of the day by a fax confirmation of all executed orders (less common in the United States) and written confirmation the following day. Each time a position is closed out, a settlement contract is sent out and then each month a summary of trades and an open position statement are sent.

There are various ways of entering an order to a futures broker, depending on the result required. The most common order is one to buy or sell a certain number of lots at a certain price. A slight variation, particularly for a larger order, is to buy or sell up to or down to a certain price slightly above or slightly below the prevailing market price.

There are also a number of other types of order, used in different circumstances. These include an 'at best' order, where the client asks the broker to obtain the best price. The client is not guaranteed a fill using this type of order. If the broker, using his discretion, decides not to trade, the client has no right to a fill. Normally, if a client has put in an order at a price and the market trades below his price on a buy order or above it on a sell order he is guaranteed an execution.

An order can also be given 'at market'. This requires the broker to go into the market and buy or sell at the best price he can at the time. This type of order is most often given in a fast-moving market where a client wants to get into the market and is more concerned with putting his position on, or closing it out, than the last point or two on the execution. It is in every broker's interest to try and get the best fill he can for a client on any discretionary or market order, and once a relationship of trust has been established the client will often find it advantageous to give some discretion to the broker.

'Stop' or 'market if touched' orders are used to limit losses or to enter the market on a technical basis. These are orders placed at a certain level which become market orders once that level is reached. Thus if the market trades at a particular price the order will be executed immediately, but not necessarily at the price given.

There are also various other orders such as 'market on close', a market order executed only during the close of the market; 'o.c.o.' (one cancels other) where two orders are entered together, usually a stop order and an ordinary one, and as soon as one is executed, the other is cancelled; 'or better' or 'not held' where a level is given but the broker is allowed to hold back if he thinks he can do better, but no fill is guaranteed; and 'g.t.c.' (good till cancelled) where the order is left in the market until it is filled, however long that might be – normally orders are cancelled at the end of the day, unless client and broker agree otherwise.

Strategies in futures trading

In this chapter we will look at the different ways the futures market can be used by the various sectors of the oil industry.

Hedging

The most straightforward form of futures trading is the hedge, the taking of a futures position equal and opposite to the physical position to be protected. A perfect hedge is virtually impossible to achieve, because of the various quality, locational and other variations between the futures and physical markets.

Probably the most common hedge is one taken against an existing physical position actually held. For example, a trader is long of a cargo of gas oil but is somewhat nervous of the price trends on the physical market. But if it is unable to sell the cargo immediately, it can sell futures instead. Then, when the physical cargo is sold, the futures are bought back.

The hedge can also be used to fix prices for futures transactions on the physical market. A gas oil consumer, for example, knows that it will have to purchase gas oil in October, but anticipates rising prices. So, earlier in the year, it can buy futures. Then, when it prices the purchase of the physical product, it sells back the futures. Or a refiner, knowing it will be producing a certain amount of product, can, having established its crude price, sell forward to guarantee a profit.

Hedging can be split into two categories, the short hedge, involving the sale of futures, and the long hedge, buying futures.

The short hedge

The most frequent users of the short hedge are: a trader long of oil but anticipating a fall in the price; a refiner that wishes to lock in a profit on processing its crude; a crude oil producer; and a supply department with possible excess product to sell, but which is unwilling to sell on the physical market, either because of price or because the product may not be forthcoming.

Futures markets are based on the idea of a standard product in standard quantities. It may not be possible to match absolutely either size or type of crude oil or product, but the nearest possible match should be aimed for. The following example illustrates this.

Example

A trader has bought a cargo of 25 000 tonnes of gas oil, but has now decided that the market is less steady than it had believed. It has already agreed the sale of the product, on a Platt's-related basis, for ten days ahead. It therefore sells futures contracts to protect against the anticipated fall in prices. When the physical cargo sale is priced, the futures are bought back.

	Physical	$/tonne	*Futures*	$/tonne
2 July	Long 25 000 tonnes	158.00	Sells 250 lots	163.00
13 July	Cargo sold	142.50	Buys 250 lots	149.00
	Physical loss	15.50	Futures profit	14.00

Net trading loss is $1.50/tonne

Thus the trader has protected itself against the fall in price seen between buying the cargo and selling it. Although the hedge was not perfect, it saved $350 000 or selling the first cargo immediately and buying again to meet the sale commitment. The cost of the futures transaction is variable, depending on the terms agreed with the broker, but would be negligible compared with the benefit.

Some of the other possible users, such as the supply department uncertain whether or not it will have excess product, are attracted to the hedge because it is easy to get out of. So, if the refiner calls to say production will be lower than expected, it is quickly possible to remove the hedge, or even turn it round if the position is reversed.

Once a hedge is put on, it does not necessarily have to be left untouched until the physical position is changed. It is possible to trade inside the hedge, perhaps buying some of the contracts back earlier and then selling them again if the price goes up. In this case there is some speculation involved, as the futures position is no longer equal and opposite to the physical position but is being changed to reflect a view of the market.

The long hedge

The long hedge can be used by a trader short of product; a distributor with future commitments; a consumer; a supply department short of product; or a refiner wishing to lock in to a crude oil price.

Example

A consumer knows that it will take delivery of 10 000 tonnes of product in two months' time, but thinks that the price will rise in the intervening period. It is unable to buy the product now, because there is no room to store it yet. So it buys 100 lots of gas oil futures on the IPE, selling them out when their physical delivery is made.

	Physical	$/tonne	Futures	$/tonne
Aug			Buys 100 lots October	164.00
Oct	Buys 10 000 tonnes	194.00	Sells 100 lots October	192.00
			Futures profit	28.00

Net cost of physical oil is $194.00 − $28.00 = $166.00

Again, the cost of the transaction will be relatively small though the fact that the hedge is held for two months makes the interest paid or assumed on the initial and variation margins greater.

The costs of dealing on the futures markets are explained in greater detail in the Appendix (p. 135). In brief, however, they depend on the terms agreed between client and broker. An assumed interest, based on loss of interest on capital which would otherwise be used elsewhere, should be used in calculating the cost of trading. Certain other forms of security, such as treasury bills, can be used in payment of initial margins.

Spreads

Spreads involve the simultaneous purchase of one contract and sale of another, in a different month or different product, to trade the differential. The actual price of the contracts becomes irrelevant; it is only the differential that is of interest.

The introduction of new futures contracts is increasing the scope of spread trading enormously. With crude oil and several products now available, it is possible to trade the crack spread, based on refinery economics, as well as the difference between the London and New York gas oil and crude oil markets, two months within one product or two different products.

The simplest spread is that in which the same market is bought for one month and sold for another. This is most often done as a speculative trade, when one month appears to be getting out of line with another in the view of the trader; but it can also be tied in with a company's physical business.

'Carrying' spreads

From time to time most futures markets see the carrying charge reflected in the prices trading in different months. In other words, the price of a forward month is greater than the price of a nearer one plus the cost of keeping the product until the forward month. When this happens, the nearer month is bought and the further one sold. The deal is closed out by taking delivery of the product off the market and putting it back in the further month. The cost of the carry is dependent on the cost of storing the material, the cost of financing the purchase and the cost of taking and making delivery on the market.

Effecting a cash and carry is virtually the same on all the oil product markets and on crude oil although the independent storage of crude oil is less common than of oil products. In all cases, calculations of costs must be based on the worst possible case. For example, a buyer taking delivery of gas oil, heating oil or gasoline from the futures market must nominate a five-day delivery range for collecting the material, but the first nomination date may be rejected by the seller. Ideally, doing the cash and carry, a buyer would nominate the last five days of the month, but rejection by the seller would mean that the latest the product could be transferred would be the 25/26 of the delivery month. (Late transfer gives the shortest possible time between payment for the products and re-delivery.) The same rule must be considered on re-delivery; the buyer may nominate the last delivery period, which can be substituted by the seller under certain circumstances, but transfer may not happen until the end of the delivery month.

Storage rates vary from installation to installation, so again the worst case must be assumed. Although the buyer on both NYMEX and the IPE may express a preference for delivery location, the choice is the seller's. A typical New York Harbor storage rate of 2 cents per gallon is used in this example.

Example

		cents/gall
April	May gasoline bought	76.00
	June gasoline sold	80.00
4 May	Delivery range 22–26 May agreed	
26 May	Delivery made by in-tank transfer	
27 May	Payment made	76.00
	Storage for one month paid	2.00
	Interest for one month at 10%	0.65
	Total outlay	78.65
25 June	Delivery made	
26 June	Payment received	80.00
	Gross profit	1.35

The carry can also be worked in reverse, when product is lent to the market for a month, or more, because the difference in value more than reflects the cost of making delivery. This is highly unusual, however, because companies normally have, and need, a certain quality of oil which is probably not the same as the future specification. By delivering better quality oil the company loses value and will almost certainly get back lower quality. It is not possible to deliver poorer quality oil than the exchange specification.

In executing either of these carrying spreads, care must be taken in making calculations and, if any volume is being traded several months forward, the interest rate should be watched closely. It is not often possible to make large profits trading this way, and a change in the interest rate or the exchange rate can soon wipe out a modest return.

The cost of the carry limits the amount by which a market can move into contango. A contango market is one where the price of the nearby month is at a discount to the further one. Backwardation, where the nearby month is at a premium to the further one, is not limited in the same way, because of the difficulty of lending oil.

Crude-product spreads

With the advent of more futures contracts, the possibilities for spread trading are opening up. In New York there is a separate ring for trading spreads between the different contracts and the exchange quotes settlement prices daily in the same way as for normal contracts. Not all spread trading is done in the spread pit; much is still traded in the individual contract rings. When a client gives a spread order, it is up to the broker which way it is executed – it can be riskier for him to use both markets simultaneously because if he is only able to execute one side and the market moves before he has done the other, he cannot give the trade to the client. But the broker may be able to get a slightly better price for the client by 'lifting legs' or trading one side of the spread before the other.

Crack spreads are a very popular trading vehicle. The most common ones are those involving one product, either heating oil, gas oil or gasoline, against crude, but there are also a large number of 3:2:1 (crude:gasoline:heating oil) and 5:3:2 spreads traded. In both cases exchange deposits are reduced.

It is impossible to get a perfect futures match to refinery output, the basic theory behind crack spreads, because of the low number of futures contracts, but the general principles remain the same. Some traders will trade crude contracts for one month against product contracts for the following, to take account of the time lag between a refiner's buying crude and having product to sell, but most tend to use the same month. The trading of two products against crude is usually a more reliable indicator of refiners' intentions, because it gives a truer reflection of the overall state of refinery economics. The boundaries of the spread's movement are harder to determine than, say, those of a cash and carry spread. For example, if refinery utilisation is very high and the crack spreads between gasoline and crude continue to widen beyond what would normally be considered a high margin, refiners are not able to increase output and the spreads will continue to widen.

When the premium of products over crude becomes wide the futures trader would sell the products and buy the crude. It does not matter whether the differential narrows because crude prices rise or product prices fall, provided that it does narrow. As with other spread trading it is the differential that is of importance not the actual price.

When the crude becomes overvalued with respect to the products, the reverse will be done – the crude sold and the products bought.

Example
NYMEX gasoline is trading at 71.50 cents/gallon, heating oil at 51.00 cents/gallon and WTI at $20.25 per barrel, giving a differential of $6.91 per barrel. The products are sold and the crude oil bought, then, when the differential narrows, the position is lifted.

Three crude oil bought	$20.25 per barrrel
Two gasoline sold	71.50 cents/gallon
One heating oil sold	51.00 cents/gallon

differential $6.91 per barrel

Later:

Three crude oil sold	$20.00 per barrrel
Two gasoline bought	68.00 cents/gallon
One heating oil bought	52.00 cents/gallon

differential $6.32 per barrel

The profit on the trade would be $0.59 per barrel less six commissions. Margins would also have to be paid.

As with all other spreads, the actual price levels of the different contracts do not matter; it is the differentials that are important. In the above examples the same result would have been obtained if the position had been lifted when crude was trading at $16.50 per barrel, gasoline at 60 cents/gallon and heating oil at 43 cents/gallon.

Arbitrage

Arbitrage is the trading of the price differential between two markets for the same or similar product: it can mean the difference between the cash market and related futures market but here we will only deal with the difference between the same product in different futures markets.

The most common arbitrages are those between NYMEX heating oil and IPE gas oil and between WTI and Brent. In order to trade the arbitrage between any two markets it is necessary for them both to be open at the same time.

Care must be taken when arbitraging between two markets to ensure that the volumes traded in each market are the same. For example, when trading the heating oil/gas oil arbitrage, four gas oil contracts are traded for every three heating oil contracts. This arbitrage also involves comparing the price of one contract priced on a volumetric basis and one on a weight basis. Different traders use different conversion factors, but perhaps the most common is that based on the IPE gas oil standard density.

Example
NYMEX heating oil is trading at a premium to the IPE gas oil of $5.00 per tonne. A trader anticipating a widening of the differential would buy heating oil and sell gas oil, being careful to maintain the correct number of contracts (three heating oil to every four gas oil). Different traders use slightly different conversion factors to obtain a heating oil price in dollars/tonne (for Europeans) or a gas oil price in cents/gallon (for US traders).

Probably the most common conversion factor is 313 gallons/tonne, the number at the IPE gas oil's standard density of 0.845 kg/litre. By multiplying the heating oil price by 3.13 the equivalent dollars/tonne price is obtained, and by dividing the gas oil price by 3.13 cents/gallon price is reached.

	$/tonne	cents/gall
Four gas oil sold	154.00	49.20
Three heating oil bought	159.00	50.80
Differential	5.00	1.60
Later:		
Four gas oil sold	148.00	47.28
Three heating oil bought	158.00	50.48
Differential	10.00	3.20

The profit is therefore $5.00 per tonne or 1.60 cents/gallon, less commissions and margin costs.

Exchange for physicals

We have dealt so far with methods that can be used for both speculative and physical business. There is also a very important trading technique specifically tied in to physical business.

An EFP, or exchange for physical, is the exchange of a futures position for a physical position. In effect, the two parties convert their futures hedges into physical positions. Sometimes it is simply used as an alternative method of delivery, but more commonly the physical transaction is the driving force behind the deal.

The major attraction of an EFP is that it separates the pricing of the oil from the physical supply. All the details relating to physical supply are agreed between the two parties, but it is agreed to price against an agreed futures market contract. The month to be used on the futures market must be determined, as must the date on which the EFP will be registered and the number of lots to be traded.

The EFP will normally be registered on or near the day the physical transfer of the oil takes place. Registration simply means the execution on the floor of the transfer of positions. The registration price is the level at which the futures position is transferred and is also used as the basis for the invoice on the physical deal. The registration price is not revealed to the market. On both NYMEX and the IPE EFPs can be registered after the contract has expired: in the case of the IPE it is a matter of a few hours; on NYMEX registration can take place the day after expiry.

The volume to be traded will normally be the agreed physical volume. Tolerance arrangements must be made separately. Some traders will EFP the total volume and then price the tolerance at the EFP price (plus or minus the differential). When the EFP is registered after the actual delivery volume is known, the exact amount will be exchanged with buyer or seller taking the tolerance risk as normal (and hedging it if thought desirable). Whichever arrangement is being made for the tolerance, it must be included in the contract.

It is also important to establish a differential or a means of agreeing a differential if the product or crude being delivered does not exactly match the futures contract. Sometimes the differential is agreed at the same time as the physical transaction, if it is relatively constant; more normally it is agreed close to the delivery, possibly using an average of a published differential over a few days. These differentials rarely cause too many problems in practice because most differentials are fairly transparent at any one moment although they vary over time. Failure to agree a differential will result in one party having a long futures position, the other a short one and no physical deal taking place.

Once the deal has been agreed, each party is free to use the futures market at any time they wish, trading in and out of positions whenever they feel it is appropriate. On the agreed day both parties notify their brokers that the EFP is to be registered, giving the number of lots and the price at which the EFP is to be transacted. This price is used to close out the futures position and is also the basis for the invoice price (plus or minus differential) for the physical deal. It is not, therefore, significant. Most EFPs are registered at the previous night's close or the current market price. (Although the price is irrelevant to the EFP transaction, it can have tax implications where, for example, physical and futures profits are taxed separately or where producers are liable to tax on their physical sales price.)

The registration of an EFP does not have to close a trader's futures position – it can create one. A physical seller, for example, who will receive long contracts with the registration of an EFP, may prefer to take the long position and sell it out when prices rise. The futures position thus created will be margined as soon as the EFP is registered.

The registration of an EFP is the only time the futures markets can be traded without open outcry. Only the number of lots and the month traded are disclosed to the market, though the exchange and the clearing house have to be told the price. The price does not have to be within the day's trading range and is not important to the exchange. What is important, however, is that EFPs are only done as part of a physical transaction. The exchanges are able to, and do, ask for documentary proof of the physical transfer.

It is important to note that it is only the futures side of an EFP that is guaranteed by the clearing house. An EFP is essentially a physical transaction and should therefore only be entered into with those other parties a trader is authorised to deal with.

Example

Company A is selling 450 000 barrels Ninian crude to Company B using the August Brent contract to price. The EFP is to be registered on 10 July at the previous day's settlement price and the differential is to be the market rate on 10 July.

Company A builds up a short position at an average price of $17.75 per barrel and Company B a long position at an average price of $16.60 per barrel. The settlement price on 9 July is $17.00 per barrel and the differential on the day is 10 cents discount.

Company A	$/bbl	Company B	$/bbl
Short futures	17.75	Long futures	16.60
EFP registered	17.00	EFP registered	17.00
Futures profit	0.75	Futures profit	0.40
Invoices B	16.90	Invoiced by A	16.90
Net sales price	17.65	Net purchase price	16.50

Thus it can be seen that both buyer and seller have a net price of their futures position less the 10-cent discount. Whatever the registration price, the result will be the same.

All these methods of using the futures markets are being constantly refined and adjusted by the industry to adapt to its needs. Most of the over-the-counter trading methods introduced to the oil market in the last decade have been developed from these methods and the options strategies discussed in Chapter 7.

On the IPE it is also possible to do an exchange for swap, or EFS. In this case, instead of exchanging the futures deal for a physical deal it is exchanged for swap. Again the exchange can ask for evidence of a swap deal.

Options

Traded options have opened up a whole new range of trading possibilities and can be used to take advantage of any view of the market – even a view that it will move sideways.

This chapter is meant to give an outline of option theory and strategies. Those wishing to study the subject more deeply will find a wide range of specialist books available. This chapter deals with exchange-traded options. An introduction to over-the-counter options (OTC) will be found in Chapter 8.

It is important to note that options, despite the limited risk they offer buyers, are not always the right instrument to use. They have a great number of uses and provide opportunities and protection not available elsewhere. But to trade options profitably it is still necessary to have a view on the market and an objective.

Options can be thought of as insurance policies: the buyer pays a premium and in return receives protection against adverse price moves while still being able to benefit from price moves in its favour. The premium varies according to the price and amount of cover required. The seller receives the premium but has to make any necessary payments to the buyer.

An option gives the buyer the right to be long (a call option) or short (a put option) of a futures contract at a specified price (the strike price) in return for the payment of a premium. The buyer has until the option expiry date, or declaration date, to decide whether or not to exercise the option. The declaration date is normally a few days before the expiry of the underlying futures contract.

Having paid the premium in full at the time of purchase, the buyer does not have to take any further action unless or until it decides to exercise its option. On exercise an option becomes a normal futures contract and is margined accordingly. If a buyer decides not to exercise the option it need do nothing and any loss is limited to the premium it paid.

The seller of the option, on the other hand, receives the premium but its risk is unlimited while its profit is limited to the premium.

A buyer will only exercise its option if it is profitable or 'in-the-money'; that is, if the market is above the strike price of a call option or below the strike price of a put option. When the market is at the strike price, the option is called 'at-the-money'. An 'out-of-the-money' option is one which would be unprofitable if exercised, that is, a put option with a strike price below the market or a call option with a strike price above the market.

Traded options are sometimes called American options to distinguish them from the older European options, rarely traded on exchanges now, which could not be traded after purchase. Traded options are fully tradable instruments and are cleared in a similar way to the futures markets, though the margining is very different. Thus anyone who has sold an option can buy it back at any time and any buyer can sell it out in an open outcry market similar to a futures market. These options can be exercised at any time, unlike OTC options which can only be exercised on expiry. In practice early exercise is rarely, if ever, justified.

The option premium is made up of two distinct parts: time value and intrinsic value. Time value is determined by the time to the expiry of the option, volatility, interest rates and supply and demand and the intrinsic value is determined by the difference between the strike price and the current market price of the underlying futures contract. An in-the-money option, which would be profitable if exercised immediately, has intrinsic value while at-the-money and out-of-the-money options do not. An in-the-money option is inevitably more expensive than an out-of-the-money one and an option with a long time to run more expensive than a short term one.

The biggest variable in the premium is the volatility. There are two measures of volatility – historical and implied. Historical volatility is calculated from past price movement and is the annualised standard deviation of the price changes in the underlying futures contract. It can be used to calculate the theoretical value of an option premium.

More significant, however, is the implied volatility, which is calculated from the option premium and is a measure of the price movement the market expects. Options are traded in an open market and are therefore subjected to the normal market laws of supply and demand, and the influence of sentiment. If traders expect more volatile trading conditions they are prepared to pay higher option premiums. Actual option premiums therefore deviate significantly from the theoretical values but can give an indication of traders' willingness to trade options at higher or lower volatility levels than historical price movements suggest.

It can happen that, in the run up to an OPEC meeting for example, the market is moving generally sideways and the historical volatility is falling but the implied volatility is increasing because the market is expecting a major price move.

Very few options are exercised. Most are not held until expiry but are sold or bought back on the market. On the last day of trading the premium of an in-the-money option is the intrinsic value and by selling an option out the trader avoids the initial and variation margin requirements of a futures position, does not have to bear the risk of the position overnight and probably saves on broker's commission.

Buying options

Option buyers pay the premium and in return receive the right to be long (call option) or short (put option) of the underlying futures contract at the strike price. There are three ways of disposing of these options. The most common method of disposal is to sell the option back to the market. This is effectively trading the premium and any profit or loss is determined by the change in the premium between purchase and sale.

Many options expire worthless: the option is bought when a trader is looking for cover at a particular price level but the market later moves away from the strike price and the option is no longer needed. If the market price at the time the option expires is far away from the strike price the option will have no value.

Finally the buyer can choose to exercise the option. The exchange is informed and the buyer becomes long or short of the market at the strike price. An option seller is then allocated the opposite transaction by the clearing house. Up to the time of expiry, part of the option's value is determined by the time the option has left to run. This means that a buyer will rarely, if ever, exercise early as this value will be lost. The profit would be greater if the option were sold back to the market.

Selling options

Most option strategies are generally looked at from the buyer's point of view because it is possible to quantify the risks and to see the potential profitability at any time. As far as the seller is concerned, it can never make a greater profit than the premium it has received. If the option is out-of-the-money it will not be exercised and the seller will have made its maximum profit, the total premium. If not, the seller's potential loss increases as the option moves further into the money. An option seller will normally have physical cover for its sales or will take cover on the futures market or buy the option back if the market moves through the strike price.

Making any trade which has limited profitability and unlimited risk may seem unattractive, but there are plenty of occasions when selling an option has considerable appeal for a physical oil trader. For instance, a producer of crude oil or products has inventory and may like to sell options to generate an income from it. If prices are, in its opinion, high it may decide to sell call options with a strike price above the current market value. If it is right and the market moves lower, its option will decrease in value, giving a profit to offset against the cost of the inventory. If it is wrong, it can buy the option back or buy futures or use its physical material as cover. It is, in effect, setting a maximum selling price for its oil.

An option seller will always gain from a decline in time value. Time value decreases throughout the life of an option but this decrease in value becomes greater towards the end of an option's life as each day represents a greater proportion of the remaining time. Thus, if nothing else changes in the market, an option seller will benefit from time passing and the time value part of the premium decreasing.

Option strategies

The only ways of trading options are buying and selling puts and calls: more complicated strategies are made up of various combinations, sometimes with a futures or physical position incorporated. Strategies can become as complicated as traders wish to make them involving any number of options, futures and physical legs. When working out some of these strategies, however, it is always worth checking to see that there is not a simpler way of achieving the same objective. Until a trader is totally familiar with the subject it is often useful to break a strategy up into its different components and work out what the result would be at different price levels.

The diagrams in this section show the profit/loss profile of the different strategies at expiry with the buyer's or seller's profile shown by a solid line. Prior to expiry the profit and loss profile is curved because of the time value remaining in the option. The closer an option comes to expiry, the closer it comes to the expiry profile.

All examples are given using crude oil options with the following premiums.

Strike $/bbl	Call premium cents/bbl	Put premium cents/bbl
$16.00	210	10
$17.00	130	30
$18.00	70	70
$19.00	30	130
$20.00	10	210

This table of premiums illustrates the way the put and call premiums behave. Assuming the market is trading at $18.00, the $17.00 put option and the $19.00 call option are both $1 out-of-the-money: they will therefore both have the same premium. Similarly the

$16.00 call and the $20.00 put are both $2.00 in-the-money and also have the same premium. This is because option premiums do not normally give any indication of the direction of market movement: prices are statistically as likely to move higher as lower.

By combining options and futures it is possible to arbitrage between different option premiums if they do move out of line. Market makers (described later) and others will trade on any short term discrepancy that appears and keep premiums in line.

Buying call

A call option gives the buyer the right to be long of the market and therefore becomes profitable when the market on expiry moves above the strike price. So a March $18 crude oil call option bought for 70 cents moves into the money when March futures move above $18.00. Between $18.00 and $18.70 the profit on the futures begins to offset the premium and the option becomes profitable when prices are above $18.70 (see Figure 7.1).

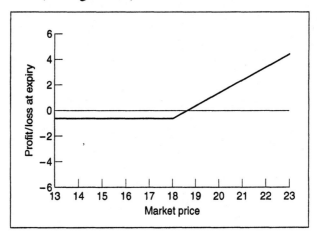

7.1 Buyer of $18 call option.

Selling call

The seller of this call option takes in the premium and provided prices remain below $18.00 will make a 70-cent profit. As soon as the price moves above $18.00 on expiry the seller will be short of the market and will therefore lose money as the market moves higher. Breakeven will be at $18.70 as the loss on the futures contract erodes the premium (see Figure 7.2).

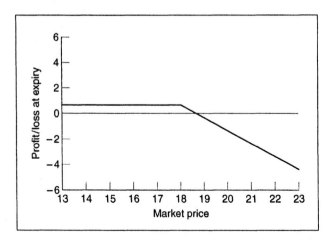

7.2 Seller of $18 call option.

Buying put

A put option gives the buyer the right to be short of the market at the strike price. The trade becomes profitable as soon as the market has fallen below the strike price less the premium paid. Thus a buyer of a

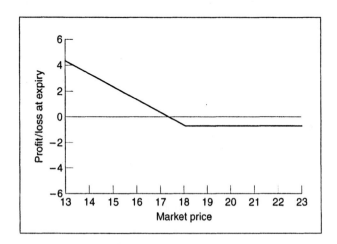

7.3 Buyer of $18 put option.

June $19.00 WTI put option for 30 cents begins to see a profit as soon as the market falls below $18.70 on expiry (see Figure 7.3). The buyer would, however, sell or exercise its option if the market were anywhere below $19.00 at expiry to recover some of the premium. It may of course sell it (or, unusually, exercise it) at any time between purchase and expiry.

Selling put

The seller of this option will be in profit provided the market remains above $18.70 (the strike price less the premium received). While the market is above $19.00 on expiry the buyer will not exercise and the seller will therefore retain the full premium. Below $18.70 the premium taken will have been offset by the loss on the futures contract (see Figure 7.4).

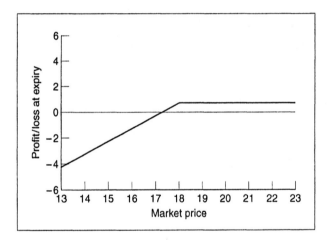

7.4 Seller of $18 put option.

Straddles and strangles

A trader looking for a significant move, but uncertain as to the direction of it, may decide to buy both puts and calls. If it buys a put and a call at the same price this is known as a straddle (or sometimes a volatility spread) but if the call has a higher strike price than the put it is known as a strangle. These trades can also be put on in anticipation of an increase in volatility as an increase in volatility will always help the buyer of an option by increasing premiums. Straddles (see Figure 7.5) and strangles have similar profit profiles. The choice between the two would be largely a matter of price.

Either of these would be sold by someone looking for a decrease in volatility, probably caused by a sideways moving market. Volatility will normally decline in a flat market although an overhanging threat may lead to an increase in demand for options and a consequent increase in volatility. A short strangle is shown in Figure 7.6. The maximum profit is obtained if the market is trading between the two strike prices on expiry.

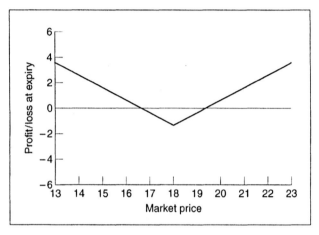

7.5 Straddle buyer (long $18 call, $18 put).

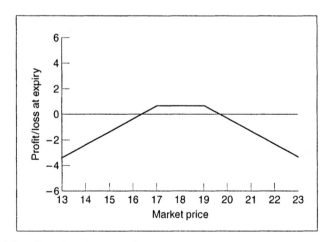

7.6 Straddle seller (short $19 call, $17 put).

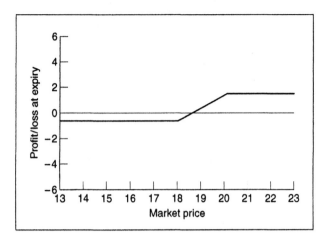

7.7 Call spread buyer (long $18 call, short $20 call).

Call spreads

Bull call spreads and bear put spreads are also commonly traded. The former is the buying of a call option and the selling of a call option with a higher strike price. It will always involve the net payment of a premium because the option being bought has a strike price closer to the market. The spread is bought when a trader is bullish for a limited move. It is also a useful way of subsidising the cost of the nearer option, particularly when high volatility makes option premiums appear expensive. By buying one and selling the other the trader is limiting profit to the difference in strike price less the premium (see Figure 7.7), but in return for giving up potential profitability is not paying for the volatility and time value (because the two call options will have the same time value and similar volatility).The maximum profit is the difference between the strike prices less the net premium paid. It is achieved if the market is at the higher strike price on expiry.

Put spreads

A bear put spread is the opposite – the buying of a put option and the selling of a put option with a lower strike price. The maximum profit of the difference in strike less the net premium is achieved if the market is exactly on the lower strike price at expiry (see Figure 7.8).

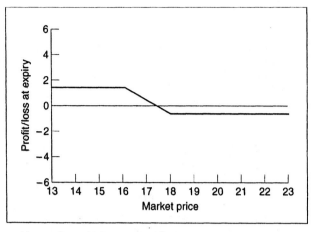

7.8 Bear spread buyer (long $18 put, short $16 put).

Fences/collars

Another way of reducing the cost of an option is to buy one option and sell the other kind, that is to buy a call and sell a put or buy a put and sell a call. This strategy is called a fence or a collar and is commonly combined with a long or short futures position. For example a crude oil producer might buy a put option to protect itself on the downside, financing this by selling a call option. This means that it has fixed a minimum selling price by buying the put but has also fixed a maximum selling price by selling the call. Between the two strike prices it would be exposed to the market. The overall profit and loss profile is shown in Figure 7.9.

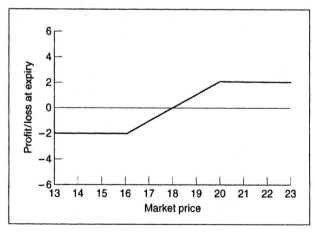

7.9 Long physical (long $16 put, short $20 call).

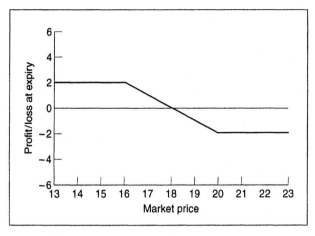

7.10 Short physical (long $20 call, short $16 put).

A company short of oil, such as an airline, would do the reverse option strategy, selling the put and buying the call, as shown in Figure 7.10. (An airline would normally do this on the over-the-counter market where jet fuel options are available.)

The strategy is popular because it can be done at little or no cost, provided that the put and call strikes are equally far from the current market price.

Other strategies

Sometimes more options are sold than bought, thus reducing the cost of the bought option but increasing the risk, because of the net short option position. These spreads are called ratio call or ratio put spreads.

There is also a strategy called a ratio backspread, which is the reverse of a normal ratio spread in that one option is sold and more than one bought. In this case a call with a lower strike is sold and more than one with a higher strike are bought. This has the effect of increasing profitability in a rising market, with limited loss (or profit depending on the initial net cost or collection of premium) on the downside. Similarly, a put ratio backspread involves selling a put with a higher strike and buying more than one with a lower strike to gain increasing profitability in a downward market. They might be used when a buyer is looking for increasing activity and higher volatility but is more confident of the direction of that move than the buyer of a straddle.

A calendar spread is the buying of an option in one month and selling one, usually with the same strike, in a further month. The effect of volatility and time value on the net premium is different from when both options are in the same month because volatility in the two months may be different and time value will be declining faster in the nearer month.

There are a number of other standard option strategies such as a butterfly (long call at x, short two calls at y, long call at z where x<y<z or the reverse for puts) or a condor (long put at v, short put at x, short put at y, long put at z where v<x<y<z or the same for calls) but these are often mathematical plays and not necessarily interesting to someone matching options to physical positions. Both the condor and the butterfly, for example, have both limited profit and limited loss and are usually entered when the theoretical and actual premiums have diverged.

Incorporating physical or futures

By building physical or futures positions into option strategies a new range of possibilities opens up. A combination of a long physical or futures position and a long put option is known as a synthetic call, because its profit/loss profile is identical to a call option. As the put option moves into the money and increases in profitability, the physical or futures position loses at the same rate. As the market rises the option is worthless but the physical or futures position increases in value dollar for dollar with the market (after the premium has been recouped).

Similarly, being short physical or futures and long a call option is a synthetic put option. As the market rises the call option profit balances out the futures or physical loss and as the market falls the physical or futures profit increases in line with the market once the premium has been accounted for.

By putting these synthetic options into the strategies explained above the desired objective can be achieved. For example, someone with a long physical position and wanting to put on a straddle will buy two put options, one to be the put leg of the straddle and one to make a synthetic call option with its physical position.

All the diagrams in this chapter show the value of the strategies at expiry. If the option position is lifted before expiry the picture is somewhat different, primarily because of the effect of time value. Anyone selling an option out before expiry will recoup some of the time value it has gained. This change is often outweighed by the change in the intrinsic value, but it does mean, for example, that a party that bought a put option because it thought the market was going down but then changed its mind should sell that option to recoup some of the loss. Someone who is short out-of-the-money options should let them expire rather than buy them back.

Delta hedging

Delta hedging is a refinement of straightforward hedging using option. Delta is defined as the rate of change in the option premium with a change in the underlying futures prices. An at-the-money option has a theoretical delta of 0.5 which means that the premium will increase or decrease at 0.5 of the change in the price of the underlying futures. A heavily in-the-money option has a delta approaching 1.0 so that any change in the underlying futures price is reflected almost cent for cent in the premium. Conversely a heavily out-of-the-money option has a delta approaching zero, meaning that a change in the underlying futures price has virtually no effect on the premium. An instantaneous reading of delta is given by all the on-line and other computer pricing models for options.

When using options to hedge it can be desirable to achieve an equivalent options profit to any physical loss. An equal volume of options and physical barrels will not give this effect prior to expiry because the option premium will not change at the same rate as the futures or physical price. It is therefore necessary to adjust the number of options to get the correct profit. If, for example, at-the-money options are being used, it will be necessary to have twice as many option barrels as actual barrels because the option premium will only move half as fast as the underlying futures.

But any price move will put the option in- or out-of-the-money and will thus alter the delta and thus the number of options necessary. As the market price, and therefore delta, changes, it is necessary to adjust the number of options at frequent intervals to maintain the correct cover. In practice, most traders will look at the position, and make any necessary changes after certain price movements.

Example
A trader holding 50 000 barrels of crude oil wants to hedge using at-the-money options on the Brent market. The current market price is $19.00 per barrel. Its requirement is for 100 put options on day 1.

	Market price	*Delta*	*Options required*
Day 1	$19.00	0.50	100
Day 2	$19.50	0.45	111
Day 3	$20.00	0.40	125
Day 4	$19.00	0.50	100
Day 5	$18.00	0.70	71

It is not only a change in the underlying futures price that affects option premiums. It is also possible to calculate how option premiums will move with changes in the volatility (vega) and time (theta). Delta itself changes over time and the effect of this can also be determined (gamma). These can all be calculated mathematically and various types of option pricing software are available for the option trader.

Market making in options

There are a number of specialist market makers on all the options markets, quoting options on a mathematical basis. They will quote bids and offers for any option at any time, using delta hedging and other methods to ensure they do not have any theoretical exposure to the market. (In practice sudden changes in price or volatility can have an effect on their positions.) They are therefore active in the underlying futures markets, constantly taking cover and building up option/futures strategies.

Over-the-counter instruments

In the late 1980s a new type of oil trading company began to emerge. Known as the 'Wall Street refiners' they were departments of the US investment banks who came into the market to introduce a variety of trading techniques and instruments, known as derivatives, many of them initially developed on the financial markets. These techniques are based on exchange-traded futures and options but can be more closely tailored to the customer's requirements. With so few exchange-traded instruments available, these new instruments were welcomed by the industry and the investment banks were soon joined by the major oil companies and some large traders as providers of the new tools.

The providers of the instruments are known as market makers. They provide bid–offer spreads on the instruments: these will be individual and anyone wishing to trade would have to check with several market makers, or use a derivatives broker, to find the best price. The difference between the bid and the offer will depend on the liquidity of the individual markets. In an active liquid products market, for example, it will normally be around $0.50–1.00 per metric tonne (MT) for the nearby months.

Over-the-counter (OTC) instruments are normally purely financial transactions: no physical delivery takes place. They are traded between two parties and so all arrangements can be freely negotiated, unlike exchange-traded instruments where everything except the price is determined by the exchange. This freedom of negotiation enables basis risk to be reduced and in some cases entirely eliminated because the terms can be matched as closely as possible to the physical requirements.

Swaps

The most straightforward of the over-the-counter instruments is a swap. This is the OTC equivalent of the futures contract. A swap is defined as the exchange of a fixed price now for a floating price at a predetermined time in the future. It enables a physical oil buyer to fix a purchase price or a physical seller to fix a selling price, in the same way that a futures contract would. In the case of a swap, however, the time at which the transaction will be reversed must be fixed in advance. When this time comes, the swap is reversed using prices published by Platt's or Petroleum Argus, the industry price reporting publications. This reversal is the equivalent to trading out of a futures position.

The reversal price is normally the monthly average of the agreed published price. Swaps can be done for longer periods, quarterly or yearly for example, but there would normally be monthly settlement. Many physical transactions, particularly those between consumers of products and their suppliers, are done at a monthly average price, making a swap an attractive hedging instrument for many consumers.

Example
An airline wishes to fix the price of its jet fuel purchases for the second quarter of the year. It approaches several swap providers and agrees to deal with one who has offered a price for the whole quarter of $185 MT. There is to be monthly settlement on contract.

At the end of each month during the second quarter the average of the Platt's quotations is calculated: if the average is greater than $185 MT the swap provider will pay the airline; if it is lower the airline will pay the provider.

Thus:

	Platt's average	Airline	Market maker
April	$190	receives $5	pays $5
May	$178	pays $7	receives $7
June	$195	receives $10	pays $10

So, whatever the price, the airline has paid $185 MT. If its physical purchase is also agreed on a Platt's monthly average (using the same Platt's quotation) the basis risk has been eliminated.

Swaps are actively traded in a number of products and crude oils. In particular, gasoline, jet fuel and fuel oil are active in the three major products markets of north-west Europe, Singapore and the US, with naphtha in the first two and gas oil in Singapore. Product swaps tend to be traded in the short and medium term with few contracts stretching forward more than a year.

Crude oil swaps can be, and are, done for longer periods. It is possible to trade Brent or WTI, for example, as far ahead as ten or even twenty years. Such swaps are unusual but could be useful, for example, to a producer wishing to guarantee income from a new well.

Swaps are generally available in any product or crude where there is an active underlying forward or futures market, or where there is a reasonable relationship with such a forward market. Market makers need to hedge their own exposure and to do this they need an instrument with which to do it.

Airlines are a major user of swaps, as are oil refiners who can do swaps on either individual product/crude differentials or on the whole refinery margin. A swap on a spread is the same as a straightforward swap except that instead of an outright Platt's or Petroleum Argus price being used, a differential between two or more published prices is employed.

CFDs

All swap contracts are contracts for difference because settlement is made by a financial transaction not by the delivery of oil. But the oil industry uses the term 'contract for difference', or CFD, for a specific type of swap contract.

Many types of physical crude oil are priced against dated Brent. (Dated Brent is described in Chapter 3.) This can make them difficult to hedge as dated Brent prices move independently of forward Brent and dated Brent itself is not a suitable hedging instrument. The industry therefore developed a means of hedging the differential between dated Brent and the first month forward Brent. This is the CFD, which is a swap on that differential.

CFDs are normally traded for calendar week periods. This means that the unwinding of the swap takes place using the Platt's quotations for a Monday–Friday period. CFDs are traded up to about six weeks forward, though some market makers are prepared to quote further out.

Example

Company X buys a cargo of Bonny Light pricing January 21–25 at dated Brent plus 50 cents and sells it at March Brent plus 40 cents. X has no absolute price exposure, because neither purchase price nor sales price is fixed, but it is exposed to the differential between dated Brent and March Brent: if dated Brent rises more than March Brent or falls less, any profit in the deal will erode or even turn into a loss.

X therefore uses a CFD to lock in to a differential. By calling several market makers, or a broker, the market level of the CFD for the week 21–25 January can be established.

Let us assume that the market is a differential of minus 20 cents (i.e. dated Brent is at a 20 cent discount to March Brent) and March Brent is trading at $18.00.

This price for dated Brent will be based on expectations of the future and not be related to the current market. X buys dated Brent at March Brent less 20 cents, or $17.80, and sells March Brent at $18.00.

By doing this it has locked in a profit on the physical deal:

Effective purchase price = dated Brent + 50 cents

                                  = (March Brent – 20 cents) + 50 cents

                                  = March Brent + 30 cents

Sales price = March Brent + 40 cents

Profit = 10 cents

When the week January 21–25 arrives, the physical cargo is priced and the CFD unwound, using the Platt's quotations for the period.

Thus:

	dated	*March*
Jan 21	$18.45	$18.70
Jan 22	$18.65	$18.75
Jan 23	$18.75	$18.70
Jan 24	$19.00	$18.85
Jan 25	$18.90	$19.00
average	$18.75	$18.80

To reverse the position X sells dated Brent at the average price and buys March Brent, also at the average.

Overall X has therefore:

CFD	Bought dated at	$17.80	Sold March at	$18.00
	Sold dated at	$18.75	Bought March at	$18.80
		$ 0.95		($ 0.80)
	Profit $0.15			
Physical				
	Bought at	$19.25		
	Sold at	$19.20		
	Loss	($ 0.05)		

Overall, the profit of $0.10 has been maintained.

Had the market moved in a different way, there may have been a loss on the CFD and a profit on the physical deal, but whatever happened the 10 cent profit is locked in.

Partials

Another commonly used instrument is known as a partial. Partials are part-cargoes of, normally, Brent or Dubai. They were introduced because of the large, 500 000 barrel, size of the forward contracts. The high liquidity of the Brent futures contract means that there is less need for a partial contract, but there are still companies which are not allowed by their own management to use futures markets and for which partial contracts are therefore useful.

The trading of partials takes place in parcel sizes of 25 000 to 50 000 barrels, or multiples thereof. It is necessary for the users of the market either to build up a whole 500 000 barrel cargo or to reverse their position before the contract moves through to the delivery period. The greater flexibility in volume is their major attraction.

Trigger pricing

Trigger pricing is, in effect, an over-the-counter EFP. It enables the user to separate price and supply and to choose the time when the price of a deal is fixed, irrespective of the time when the physical transfer takes place. As with swaps, trigger pricing deals are done with a market maker and are normally financial deals only, though occasionally the market maker will take or make physical delivery.

An agreement is made to price the physical cargo against a reference crude oil or product: for example, it might be Bonny Light crude priced at February Brent plus 40 cents/barrel. As with any deal, a volume of oil must be agreed and a minimum volume for each trigger. Finally, a time frame must be agreed: this is in effect a closing date for the pricing of the deal.

Example
Company A agrees to sell a 500 000-barrel cargo of Forties crude oil, loading March 8–10 to market maker B at April Brent plus 10 cents. The price can be triggered any time before 15 March in minimum quantities of 50 000 barrels. At any time between the time the deal is agreed and 15 March A can call B and get a quote on April Brent. If the quote is acceptable a deal is done for the agreed quantity. The contract will also include a fall-back price so that if agreement is not reached on any day the Platt's price can be used, at A's request.

Assuming the deal was done in mid February, the calculation may look like the following:

Date	Volume	Price (Brent plus 10 cents)
Feb 20	50 000 bbls	$18.00
Feb 24	150 000 bbls	$18.10
Feb 27	100 000 bbls	$17.85

Feb 28	100 000 bbls	$17.65
Mar 10	100 000 bbls	$17.95

The average price for the deal is therefore $17.92. If it is a physical deal B will pay A $17.92. If there is no physical aspect to the transaction, it becomes a swap transaction and will be reversed at the average of Platt's or Petroleum Argus over an agreed time period.

The advantages of trigger pricing deals are that users do not have to rely on the market at a specific time to price their sales or purchases. Instead they can choose when to fix the price. Should they wish, pricing can continue long after the cargo has lifted, provided that a suitable contract month has been agreed for the reference price. (The reference price can be changed by agreement within the lifetime of the contract.) Some cargoes have not been finally priced for more than a year after loading. Alternatively, the price could be fixed long in advance.

Options

The other main area of activity in the over-the-counter market is in options. There are many variations on traditional option strategies available, made up of various combinations of puts, calls and swaps. The main difference between OTC options and exchange-traded options is that the former are bilateral agreements and all the terms can be negotiated, whereas all terms, except price, are fixed by the exchanges for their options. Another important difference is that, with few exceptions, OTC options cannot be exercised early, but this is rarely an attractive choice for the buyer in any case.

Many OTC options use an average monthly price for exercise rather than the single expiry day used on futures markets. This use of an average price generally gives them lower implied volatilities than exchange-traded options, making them cheaper. They also match more closely with the standard swap contracts. As with most other OTC contracts they are purely financial instruments, settled by cash transfer.

The terminology used on the OTC market tends to differ from exchange-traded options, with puts generally known as floors and calls as ceilings. But the theory is otherwise the same as that described in Chapter 7.

A very popular strategy on the OTC market is the costless collar. This is the purchase of a call and sale of a put or purchase of a put and sale of a call with the same premium. Looking at the former type, as used by consumers, this gives a maximum purchase price at the call strike, but also a minimum purchase price, the put strike.

For example, if a jet fuel buyer, an airline, buys a costless collar with strikes of $185 MT for the call and $170 MT for the put, it would have a net purchase price as shown in Figure 8.1.

If the market price is between $170 MT and $185 MT the buyer would pay the market price for the jet fuel and both sides of the option deal would expire worthless. If the market is above $185 MT the call option will be exercised, giving a profit to offset against the physical price, keeping the net maximum paid to $185 MT, however far the market rises.

If, however, it falls below $170 MT the put option will be exercised by the market maker and the airline will pay less for the physical jet fuel but will have to pay the market-maker the difference between the strike price and the current market price. Thus the airline will not benefit from prices below the strike.

Thus, the cost of the protection against rising prices, the call option, is the inability to benefit from lower prices.

Costless collars will have strike prices more or less equidistant from the current market price when the option is taken out. There will

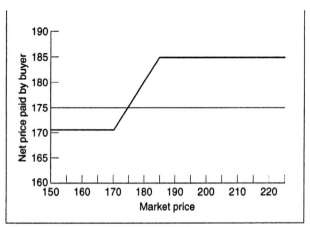

8.1 Costless collar strategy.

be a bid–offer spread built into the quote, however, leading to a slight shift in the strikes.

Swaptions

A swaption is an option on a swap. The buyer of the option pays a premium for the right to choose at a later date whether or not to take the swap contract. As with most swaps, they will normally be for a period of a month, a quarter or a year and the option will have to be declared, or exercised, before the period begins.

Embedded options

The user of swaps can choose to have an embedded option incorporated in the deal. This means that the market maker has the option to extend the period of the swap, or to change the volume of it, in return for giving the user a better price. In other words, a consumer of, say, fuel oil might be looking for a swap for 5000 tonnes/month for the third quarter of the year. The market maker might offer a price of, say, $100 MT for the normal third quarter swap. But it might be able to offer, say, $98 MT in return for giving the market maker the right to increase the volume to 10 000 tonnes/month; or $97.50 MT to extend it to six months rather than three.

The improvement in the price is the premium the market maker pays for the option to change the period or volume.

Another type of embedded option is where the user receives a worse price in return for buying not only the normal swap but an option to participate in advantageous price moves. In a normal swap contract the user locks in to a price, thus the user of a swap to fix a selling price will not benefit from rising prices because any rise above the swap price will have to be paid to the market maker. But if an embedded call option has been included in the price, it can benefit from rising prices. The user can choose the degree of participation, from 0 to 100 per cent, paying the premium accordingly.

Tailor-made instruments

Market makers are able to combine different types of market into their strategies. For example, all instruments can be offered in local currencies, in cases where the currency is actively traded on the financial markets and can be hedged.

Over-the-counter instruments can be more flexible than exchange-traded instruments because the terms can be negotiated between the two parties. But they are bilateral contracts so they cannot be traded freely in open markets, as futures contracts can be. It is normally possible to trade out of any position, but it may be necessary to make the opposite transaction with a different market maker because the price may be more attractive.

There is no formal margining of OTC instruments, though in many cases there will be some form of staged payments to prevent either side becoming too exposed to the other. This is particularly true of some of the longer term instruments which may have a lifetime of twenty years or so.

OTC instruments are also attractive to those who cannot, for company policy or other reasons, trade exchange futures and options. Difficulties with foreign exchange controls, which can cause problems for those wishing to use futures, can also sometimes be overcome by using a market maker rather than an exchange.

Many companies with oil price exposure but not directly involved in oil trading, including not only consumers of oil but also those on the crude oil production and refining sides of the industry, prefer to fix prices using the more flexible instruments than to manage the basis risk inherent for many in using exchange-traded instruments.

The two markets are closely intertwined: market makers use futures and forward markets extensively to hedge their positions. Most of them will take positions on the markets, but much of their exposure must still be hedged.

How the oil industry can use the futures markets

In this chapter we examine some of the different ways in which the oil industry can use the futures and OTC markets to complement its physical trading activities. In fact, each company using the markets develops its own preferred trading methods from these basic theories and will analyse its risks and consequent futures requirements in a slightly different way, just as companies do on the physical markets.

In all the examples given in this chapter it is assumed that hedges and other futures positions are left in place until the related physical position has been disposed of. In practice, many futures positions are not left in place but are lifted and replaced, in whole or in part, as the user's opinion of the market changes. A perfect hedge applied throughout a physical position's life would indeed virtually eliminate risk but it would also remove the opportunity for increasing profit. Most traders wish to take advantage of price moves in their favour while gaining protection against an adverse move. Futures and options markets should theoretically make it possible to do this, but only when traders 'read' the market correctly.

Backwardation and contango can cause major difficulties for all those using the markets. Backwardation, where the nearer month is trading at a premium to the further one, makes forward hedging look unattractive for producers, while a contango market, where the nearby month is lower than the further one, makes it look expensive to consumers. It is a further factor that must be taken into account when choosing which instrument to use to hedge and what proportion of the exposure to hedge.

Supply department

Supply departments in any large company have, by their very nature, an unpredictable life. They can find themselves unexpectedly long or short of product, or facing sudden changes in stocks or production levels. As they constantly try to balance these supply and demand fluctuations, the futures and options markets can be used to overcome some of the problems. One of the main advantages of futures and options trading is the ease with which positions can be adjusted or removed altogether. This ease is partly the high level of liquidity and partly the administrative ease of handling futures. For example, if a position is taken on the futures markets and then removed, the position can be closed out and the deal is closed. If the same protection is taken on the cash market and later closed, the department may still have to become involved in nominations, book outs and other administrative details even if the cargo deal was reversed some weeks previously.

Occasionally product can be bought from the market one month and sold back the following month at a premium sufficient to cover the costs of storage and delivery. It is rarely possible to make much profit on this trade, but it can be used to make better use of spare storage capacity.

Trading the cash and carry, as this is called, should be prefaced by careful calculation of the costs involved as interest rate changes and, in Europe, currency fluctuations can eliminate the potential profitability of the trade. If a cash and carry is being done some way forward, currency and interest rates should be fixed at the time the deal is done. An example is given in Chapter 6 (page 67).

Although there are additional costs of delivery arising from the physical movement of the product, these have to be calculated on a case-by-case basis because different factors come into play. For example, the product to be delivered may already be in an acceptable installation or it may have to be moved.

It is also possible to 'lend' material to the market by doing the cash and carry the other way round. This is less common, however, because the oil may be of higher, or lower, quality than the exchange contract and the user would be either giving away some value or would be unable to deliver.

A supply department may also wish to trade options against any product it may have in store. By selling call options it can generate income from its stocks. Although it will effectively be putting a maximum value on the stock, it will have the necessary cover in an upward price movement. It would only sell options if it felt the market was likely to move lower or remain more or less unchanged. In a flat market it would stand to gain not only from decreasing time value (which always works to the seller's advantage) but also from the decreasing volatility.

Example

Prices have risen steadily in recent weeks but have begun to show signs of instability. A supply department, required to maintain its physical gas oil stock levels, might wish to gain an income stream by selling gas oil calls with a strike price slightly above the market. With the market trading at $155 in mid April, the department might sell $160 call options for July at $5.80 per tonne. Prices drift lower over the next few weeks and the option is not exercised on expiry, when July futures are trading around $143.

The supply department would therefore have received an income of $5.80 per tonne (less commission and financing costs) to offset against the drop in value of its stocks. Had prices risen through $160, it could have bought back the option or used the short position effectively created to hedge its stocks, depending on its view of the market.

The income generated would not have been equal to the drop in value of the stocks unless the department had chosen to delta hedge, in which case the options would have been bought and sold repeatedly to maintain full dollar-for-dollar cover (see Chapter 7).

If the department had chosen this route, the sequence of events could have looked as follows (for each 100 tonnes in stock):

	Delta	Options required	Number bought or sold
Day 1	0.6	1.67	1.67
Day 2	0.55	1.82	0.15
Day 3	0.65	1.54	0.28

The frequency of adjusting the position can be determined by the user to maximise protection without taking all its time and costing too much in commission. Some people choose to adjust their positions every day and others once a week or after a certain move in the delta.

A supply department might also use futures to take cover against a change in its physical position.

Example
Company B's supply department receives a call from its refinery to say that production problems have meant a shortfall in gasoline availability. The supply department had already sold the material and will now have to buy gasoline on the open market. But it fears that prices are rising and will rise further before it is able to find suitable material.

So, while it is looking for suitable gasoline to buy, Company B goes on to the futures market and buys the equivalent amount of futures. When it finds the physical material it will sell out its futures contracts (or enter into an EFP transaction).

Futures		Physical	
	cents/gallon		cents/gallon
Buy futures	69.45	(trading at)	67.65
Sell futures	70.30	Bought at	68.90
Profit	0.85		

The futures profit can then be offset against the physical price to give a net price of 68.05 cents/gallon. Although this price is a little higher than the physical price when the futures were bought, this has resulted from a change in the differential between the appropriate physical grade and the futures market, known as the basis.

A supply department might also choose to sell some or all of its material on an EFP basis. Using an EFP enables any futures market user to separate the pricing of a contract from the physical supply of the product or crude.

Example
The supply department of Company C wishes to re-establish term supply contracts with Company D but does not want to enter into

fixed price or variable pricing arrangements based on published price information. Using an EFP it agrees to sell Company D 4.0 million US gallons of heating oil per month, prices to be fixed on the basis of the NYMEX heating oil contract prices for that month. All the physical contract details are agreed as normal and it is agreed that an EFP for 95 lots of heating oil will be registered on the last trading day for each month. The EFP will be registered at the previous night's settlement.

Each month, Company C will decide when it wishes to price its sales. It has agreed a premium of 25 points to the NYMEX for locational reasons. Its net sales price could be calculated as follows:

Futures		*Physical*	
	cents/gallon		cents/gallon
Sold at	51.00		
EFP registered	49.00	Company D invoiced	49.25
Futures profit	2.00		

The net sales price is therefore 51.25 cents/gallon, equivalent to the 51.00 cents/gallon futures price plus the 25-point premium.

The price at which the EFP is registered is irrelevant because it is also the price at which the physical deal is invoiced. In the above example, if the EFP had been registered at 55.00 cents/gallon, the futures loss would have been 4.00 cents/gallon, but the physical sales price would have been 55.25 cents/gallon and the net price would still have been 51.25 cents/gallon.

Using an EFP both buyer and seller can choose the time to fix the price. The two prices are independent and unknown to the other party.

The producer

Crude oil producers are always worried about falling prices. They can use the futures and options markets as a straightforward hedging medium or to fix a minimum price. If a producer is convinced that the market is going to fall, it can simply sell futures or fix the selling price using a swap. Then, if it is right, it will have a futures profit to add to the lower income it will receive for its oil, giving it a net price close to where it sold futures. Any imperfections of the hedge will result from the basis risk between the crude it produces and the futures or swap it uses and any difference between the pricing periods and mechanism of the physical sale and the futures or swap contract.

If it is wrong about the direction, however, and the market rises, it will lose out on the upside benefit for as long as the hedge position is in place. By buying options it will be able to participate in any upward move while obtaining protection against a downward one. As with anyone buying options, producers need to consider what they are trying to achieve and how much they are prepared to spend to achieve it. Much of this decision will depend on their view of the market. If they are bearish for a major move, they may like to simply buy puts. They could also consider buying puts and selling calls to reduce the cost, or doing a collar on the OTC market. But if they are bearish for a limited move they could buy a bear put spread (see Chapter 7) to reduce their outlay by selling a lower strike put than the one they are buying.

Producers are often sellers of call options as well as buyers of puts. If they feel the market is overvalued they can sell call options either at-the-money or just out-of-the-money. This way they receive an income from the premium. This does not, however, provide any protection against a downward move and the effect is to fix a maximum selling price at the strike price plus the premium while the options positions are still open.

The EFP is also a very useful tool for an oil producer. It can agree a contract with its customer and then use the futures market to price the deal. The differential between the crude it is selling and the crude traded on the futures market will have to be agreed, as will the date of registration. By using the EFP mechanism, a producer can agree a term supply contract with each delivery priced using the futures market.

Example
Producer A agrees to sell a cargo of 450 000 barrels of Ninian crude to Refiner B each month for the next year. The cargoes will be priced on the following month's contract on the IPE Brent contract (because the Brent contracts expire in the middle of the month before delivery) and the EFP will be registered on the bill of lading day or the last trading day of the contract, whichever is

first, at the previous day's settlement. The differential will be the five-day average around the bill of lading day as published by Screen Services. Using the March delivery as an example and assuming the EFP will be registered at $17.40 and the differential is 10 cents discount:

Producer A	$/barrel	Refiner B	$/barrel
Sells 450 Brent at	17.75	Buys 450 Brent at	16.80
EFP registered at	17.40	EFP registered at	17.40
Futures profit	0.35	Futures profit	0.60
Invoices B		Invoiced by A	17.30
(EFP price – 10c)	17.30		
Futures profit	0.35	Futures profit	0.60
Net price	17.65	Net price	16.70

In both cases, therefore, it can be seen that the net price is the price of the original futures contracts less the differential.

Producers may also like to use trigger pricing. In this case the producer will agree with the buyer to sell a cargo of crude, to be priced at seller's option over a fixed period. A reference crude, differential, time period and minimum size for each trigger will be determined. Then the seller will call the market maker when it wants to price the cargo in whole or in part. At this point the price will be fixed and the market maker will take any hedging action it considers necessary.

Market makers will sometimes sit between buyer and seller of a cargo so that each side can trigger the deal when it feels the time is appropriate.

The refiner

Refiners have to face constant price fluctuations in the price of both crude and products making any planning of the future costs very difficult. There have been occasions in recent years when refinery profits are good, but there have also been long periods of tight margins. Refiners have therefore become active users of the futures and OTC markets to remove some of the uncertainties.

Futures markets can be used to lock in a future crude purchase price, a product selling price or both. Refiners, however, are interested in the differential between product and crude prices, the refinery margin, not the absolute level. If the refiner has already established its crude oil price, it may wish to sell products forward to fix the margin, but if it has not it will be more interested in looking at forward margins.

Using futures markets alone is difficult because there are too few contracts to give full cover to the refiner. Gasoline, heating oil and crude on NYMEX can give a US refiner cover over most of the barrel, but European refiners have only gas oil and crude and elsewhere there are no active exchange contracts.

A refiner looking to hedge must then decide whether it wishes to hedge some of its products with futures and others in a different marketplace. The NYMEX gasoline market, for example, can provide protection against major adverse price moves in Europe, but it is a completely different market reacting to different influences.

Example

In January a refiner buys 100 000 barrels of WTI for $19.80 per barrel. It is worried that prices will fall by early March when it will be looking to sell the products on the spot market. As a US refiner, it is able to use both the gasoline and the heating oil markets on NYMEX and therefore hedge around 70 per cent of its output.

January
Buys WTI for $19.80 per barrel
Sells gasoline futures at 61.00 cents/gallon
Sells heating oil futures at 51.40 cents/gallon

March
Buys gasoline futures at 60.00 cents/gallon (1.00 cents/gallon profit)
Sells physical gasoline at 59.90 cents/gallon
Buys heating oil futures at 51.00 cents/gallon (0.40 cents/gallon profit)
Sells physical heating oil at 50.90 cents/gallon

This gives an effective gasoline cash price of 60.90 cents/gallon and an effective heating oil price of 51.30 cents/gallon.

The refiner might decide not to sell the products forward, perhaps because it thinks the market will rally. But it might want to take some cover, so it could buy put options in the product markets, so that it could take advantage of any upward move in the market but be protected against a downward move.

For example, with prices similar to those in the above example, the refiner might decide that instead of selling on the gasoline and heating oil markets, it will buy 60-cent gasoline puts and 50-cent heating oil puts. Then, if the market falls below these levels it will exercise its options (or take the profit by selling the options out) but if it rallies it will abandon the options.

The refiner might also decide to sell call options because it thinks the market will be generally stable and option volatility will decline. It would then receive the option premium and use the physical material as cover in which case it would have set a maximum selling price of the strike price plus the premium it received.

If the crude price is unknown the refiner can use the crack spread to fix the margin. The crack spread is the buying of crude and the selling of an equal number of product contracts or vice versa. In one pit on the NYMEX floor the crack spreads (either three crude, two gasoline, one heating oil or five crude, three gasoline and two heating oil) are quoted as differentials. The actual prices are fixed later. As with all spread trading the actual price levels are unimportant, it is only the differential that is important.

Example

A refiner wants to hedge its WTI-related purchases and product sales ahead because it can see an attractive refinery margin built in to the futures prices. So, during February, it buys June Brent and sells July heating oil and gasoline. When the physical crude purchase is priced, it sells the Brent futures. Then, when it prices the physical product sales, it buys back the product futures contracts. It will sell three gasoline and two heating oil for every five crude contracts as this most closely matches its product slate.

Futures	*Physical*
Now	

5 WTI bought at $18.40 per barrel
3 gasoline sold at 60.00 cents/gallon
2 heating oil sold at 54.60 cents/gallon
(paper refining margin $5.89 per barrel)

Futures	Physical
Later	
5 Brent sold at $17.00 per barrel	Bought at $17.00 per barrel
3 gasoline bought at 54.00 cents/gallon	Sold at 53.75 cents/gallon
2 heating oil bought at 50.00 cents/gallon	Sold at 50.20 cents/gallon
(paper refining margin $5.02 per barrel)	(margin $4.97 per barrel)

By executing this trade the refiner has given itself a crack spread profit of $0.87 per barrel to give a total margin of $5.84 per barrel, virtually the same as that originally fixed, although the actual margin has fallen to $4.97 per barrel.

A refiner can also use EFPs both to buy crude and sell products and can enter trigger pricing deals. Perhaps the simplest way for the refiner to hedge, however, is by using a tailored refinery margin swap on the OTC market. A market maker will quote a margin swap based on the refiner's own product slate. The refiner can then lock into a full margin, whenever the prices look attractive.

The refiner will call the market maker and will give some details about the product slate. Each product will be priced against an active underlying market, where the market maker can hedge, as with any other swap. Similarly, the crude oil will be priced relative to Brent or whatever other marker crude the refiner chooses. The product and crude prices will then be combined to give a margin and a straightforward swap contract agreed.

Settlement will normally be monthly, so at the end of each month the margin will be recalculated using the published prices for the month. If the margin is greater than that fixed the refiner will pay the market maker and if it is smaller the refiner will be paid. In this way the margin has been locked in.

It is also possible to trade an option on a refinery margin so that the refiner can maintain participation in any improvement in margins.

The traders

Traders were the first sector of the oil industry to trade the futures markets actively and continue to be a major part of the market. Some use the futures markets to add to or as an alternative to their physical positions rather than as a hedging vehicle, transferring some of their speculative trading away from the physical market because of the administrative ease of futures with no shipping and locational problems.

Looking at their use of the futures markets as a complement to their physical activities, however, hedging is probably the largest use, as with other sectors of the industry. If a trader holds a long physical position, for example, and fears that prices are falling, it can sell futures as an alternative to selling the physical cargo.

With the physical market being very transparent, other traders often know the placing of cargoes and know what a particular trader has a need to sell or buy. The trader can then find that it is unable to find another party wishing to trade at an acceptable price. But if it is hedged on the futures market it can afford to wait longer before making a physical deal. The cargo need not become distressed. The confidentiality of the futures market can be a major attraction in a case like this. Later, the trader may decide that rather than lift the hedge it will trade the physical cargo on an EFP basis and use the hedge position as the futures position for the EFP.

Again the trader has to decide which futures market to use. If it has a strong opinion about the relative strength of one market over another, it may decide not to hedge in the nearest equivalent market but to trade a different one and try and take advantage of the differential as well as hedge the cargo. This will probably make a subsequent EFP impossible, but may have some attraction, particularly if the cargo under consideration does not have an equivalent futures market. For example, someone with a European gasoline cargo might well decide that Brent provides a better hedge than the NYMEX gasoline market and will therefore use Brent.

Example

A trader has a cargo of gasoline in north-west Europe and is concerned about falling prices. It cannot find a satisfactory buyer, so decides to sell futures. It looks at the NYMEX gasoline market, but decides that this market is much stronger than the European market and it will not therefore provide much protection against falling prices. The cargo is not suitable for export to the United States so the option of sending it across the Atlantic is not there. So the trader decides to sell an equivalent quantity of Brent futures.

When it finds a buyer for the physical cargo, it may try to do an EFP against the Brent or may, more probably, simply lift the hedge.

Futures	*Physical*
Sold Brent $17.20 per barrel (equivalent price $143.28 per tonne)	Long gasoline $208.00 per tonne
Bought Brent $16.70 per barrel (equivalent price $139.16 per tonne)	Sold gasoline $202.00 per tonne

The trader has therefore made a profit of $4.12 per tonne to offset against the $6.00 loss made on the physical market. So although the hedge was not perfect, it has provided some cover in a falling market.

Even if there is a futures market in the product or crude the trader wants to trade, the relationship between the futures price and the physical price will vary from time to time. As expiry approaches the two prices must converge if the market is mature, but at other times there is a differential known as the basis. A trader hedging on the futures market is assuming basis risk, that is the risk that the differential will vary and the degree of cover provided will therefore change.

The differential between the futures and physical price for the same commodity can provide a useful trading opportunity. The trader can trade this differential in the same way as any other: buying the 'underpriced' product and selling the other. For example, it might decide to buy futures and sell the physical product because the physical product prices are relatively strong. These opportunities are usually short-lived and the profits are unlikely to be large.

It is important to be certain that the difference in price does not reflect an important difference in the two products. For example, the physical gas oil price may be higher in the short term because of bad weather preventing Russian gas oil getting into north-west Europe. If this delay is likely to continue into the delivery period of the exchange, the futures price will reflect the problem; if not, then the physical price for immediate delivery will increase but the futures will not. This means there is a difference between the two products and that difference is reflected in the price. This would not give a good trading opportunity to most traders.

Inter-month spread trading can also provide useful opportunities. Although the cash and carry (buying one month and selling a later one, settling out the trades by taking delivery one month and making it the next) is eagerly watched for and profits are limited, it can produce some profit particularly for those with access to cheap storage or who have storage unused.

The most important point to check in this trade is the exact delivery mechanism as this can make all the difference between profit and loss. In particular, delivery timing is usually at buyer's option so it cannot be assumed that a buyer will take product at any one time.

Another switch that the traders watch for is the arbitrage between NYMEX and the IPE, either the heating oil/gas oil or Brent/WTI spread. These relationships vary enormously depending on weather conditions, local production and consumption levels and sentiment.

When doing the heating oil/gas oil arbitrage the trader must decide what conversion factor it wishes to use to convert the heating oil price to dollars per tonne or the gas oil price to cents/gallon. The exact differential is not important provided that the same one is used throughout the trade and for assessing past performance. Probably the most popular conversion is 313 gallons/tonne (the conversion at the standard gas oil density of 0.845 kg/litre) though 310 and 309.54 are also popular.

It is also necessary to trade the same quantity of product on each market, which means trading four gas oil contracts to every three heating oil contracts because of the difference in size.

Example

The February arbitrage has been trading in a $3.00–9.00 range and a trader believes the potential for moving out of this range is small. When it comes back towards the lower end of the range, therefore, the trader decides to buy heating oil and sell gas oil. As it widens out again it then takes the position off as the price approaches the top of the range. In this case, there is no question of taking delivery of either market so the fact that the arbitrage does not reflect the cost of transport is not important.

IPE	$/tonne	cents/gallon	*NYMEX*	cents/gallon	$/tonne
4 gas oil sold	157.00	50.16	3 heating oil bought	51.20	160.25
4 gas oil bought	163.00	52.08	3 heating oil sold	54.65	171.05
Loss	6.00	1.92	Profit	3.45	10.80

The net profit on the trade is therefore $4.80 per tonne or 1.53 cents/gallon, less the cost of trading.

One point worth noting is that almost all the sharp movements of the arbitrage have seen a rapid rise in the NYMEX premium rather than a rapid decrease. This is largely because the NYMEX market tends to react more strongly, in the short term at least, to changes in sentiment.

Many traders will get involved in processing deals and other aspects of refining. They will therefore use the various trading methods open to refiners, particularly crack spreads and refinery margin swaps. More recently, many traders have been developing upstream or downstream activities and moving away from some of the more openly speculative areas that formerly constituted their main activity. They may therefore become involved in any trading methods applicable to those areas.

Traders can also use options, either as an alternative to futures or as a means of speculation. They can use any of the options strategies outlined in Chapter 7 and may be particularly interested in some of the volatility strategies.

Traders also use the over-the-counter markets, particularly for any longer term contracts they may have. Crude traders are very active users of the CFD market.

The marketing department

The main aim of the marketing department of a major company is to expand its company's market share while maintaining profitability. The futures market can help such a department lock into profit margins over a longer time and offer fixed prices on to its customers. A number of customers, particularly large public bodies and manufacturers, are attracted by fixed prices so they can work within their budget.

Of course, the fixed price is unlikely to be the best price, when the time comes, for both parties. It will either be below the price on the market at the time or above it. But the advantage comes from knowing what it is going to be in advance. And over a long period it is likely that an average price will be achieved by both sides. This may not, however, be seen for some time and it is difficult for any purchaser to explain why, despite keeping within its budget, it has paid above the market price. There is therefore always a degree of compromise about fixing prices forward.

It is necessary for marketing departments outside the United States, which frequently operate in local currency, to fix their currency exchange rates at the same time as the oil price. This can make the over-the-counter markets particularly attractive because the exchange rate and oil price can be linked.

The simplest method is to buy futures or a swap and use that price as the basis for selling forward. This is effectively a simple hedge.

Example
In April, Company A buys a gas oil swap at $154.00 per tonne for November. It then sells the product on to its buyer at a price based on this (fixing its currency at the same time). Come November the average Platt's price of gas oil has risen to $173.00 per tonne and the marketing department is charged that price by the refinery.

Swap	$/tonne	Physical	$/tonne
Buys November	154.00	Sells to customer	158.00
Sells November	173.00	Buys from refinery	173.00
Profit	19.00	Loss	15.00

The marketing department has achieved a net profit of $4.00 per tonne on the deal, exactly the figure built into the price to its customer based on the swap.

On the inland markets, monthly average prices are a very common way of pricing, making the swaps market very attractive. A swap can be simulated by trading futures daily, but realistically this would require a large volume to be traded.

Rather than actually buy futures, the marketing department might decide to use options, particularly if it thinks the price might fall. Using the same example, the department might decide to buy November call options with a $155.00 strike. This would probably cost it several dollars, because it is at-the-money and some months forward. It then becomes a matter of trying to balance out the risk reward ratio of the transaction.

If the department did decide to take the option route, it would only exercise the option or sell it out if the price was above $155.00. If it was below it would simply buy the product from its refinery at the market price and sell it on to its customer at the agreed price.

The distributor and large consumer

Both distributors and large consumers may wish to fix their buying prices in advance by buying swaps, or futures, against their planned requirements. As with the marketing department it is necessary to fix the currency exchange at the same time if appropriate. Some distributors have found such forward price fixing, passed on to their customers, a good marketing tool.

Unless consumers are very large they may find that entering the futures or swaps market themselves is unnecessary, indeed undesirable because of the volumes involved, but they can achieve the same protection from their supplier.

Futures are not a good way of buying forward for those in countries where the selling price of oil products is fixed by the government.

For those consumers and distributors who buy their products on a spot-related basis, however, futures and swaps can be a useful tool. When a consumer or distributor finds the price of the oil product attractive, either because it fears an upward move or because the price is at or below the budgeted price and it wishes to guarantee some of its purchases at that level it will simply fix the price using a swap or futures. Then, when the time comes to price the physical delivery from the supplier, the swap will be reversed or it will sell the futures. If prices have risen, it will have a futures profit to offset against the higher price of the physical oil.

Instead of buying futures, the consumer or distributor may like to look at buying options, which will protect it against a major upward move in prices but allow it to benefit from any fall in values. In this case the company would buy call options with a strike price at the appropriate level. When looking at option purchases in this way it is necessary to establish what cost the company is prepared to pay for what degree of cover.

Some companies prefer to allocate a fixed sum of money while others prepare to match volumes. Some prefer to buy at-the-money options, while others prefer to buy a larger number of out-of-the-money options, or the same number at a lower cost. If the market rises the value of the out-of-the-money call options will also rise, though not as fast as the nearby ones (see Chapter 7). But out-of-the-money options will often have a lower implied volatility and therefore can be seen as 'better value'. As with most things, the user has to make its choice. Buying call options will enable the consumer or distributor to fix its maximum buying price at the strike price plus the premium paid.

Exchange or OTC?

There is no right answer to the question of whether to trade on the exchanges or over-the-counter. All users of the market have to assess the various advantages and disadvantages on a deal-by-deal basis. In most cases the decision is made by looking at basis risk. Those hedging products or crudes that have futures contracts will normally use them, but many hedging other types of crude or product prefer to pass as much as possible of the basis risk to a market maker. Many of the larger users of the market will use both markets at different times.

Over-the-counter instruments can be more closely tailored to the user's requirements, while all terms, except price, of exchange-traded instruments are fixed by the exchange. OTC contracts are bilateral, unlike exchange contracts which can be freely traded on the market floor. This means that it is not as easy to get in and out of an OTC contract as a futures contract, though market makers will normally quote for the closure of a trade.

Futures exchanges are strictly regulated under the relevant government's law. OTC markets are subject to normal trading law, but there are no specific regulations at present, though there are various ideas under discussion. Futures contracts are also secured by the clearing houses. They are fully margined on a daily basis, unlike OTC contracts which may have some form of staged payments and will normally require a letter of credit. Commissions are payable on futures contracts, whereas on the OTC markets the market maker's profit is built in to the bid–offer spread on the different instruments.

Technical analysis

Technical analysis is the study of price in the marketplace with a view to determining how people react to given price levels. History and an element of psychology enable the technical analyst to make certain predictions about the direction of price movement in the future and, in certain circumstances, to predict how far prices will move.

Technical analysis was first put forward by Charles Dow, who also started the first stock market index. It is based on three basic tenets. First, and perhaps most important, is that market action discounts everything. This means that anything that is known about a commodity is reflected in its price: all supply and demand changes and all expected changes in supply and demand are reflected in the price buyers will pay or sellers will accept. The second tenet is that prices move in trends, rather than in an entirely random way. And finally, history repeats itself. This is a statement of human nature: generally people are happier when they understand from a study of the past what is happening in the present and will take place in the future.

The technical analyst is looking for three things: are prices moving sideways (i.e. not changing much), are they trending up or down or are they changing direction? It is important to remember that major price moves will always be driven by changes in the fundamentals of the market, such as supply disruptions, but in the absence of major news, technical analysis enables the user to make predictions about price movement.

An oil industry user of the market will probably not use charts to determine what to do in the market, but may well change the timing of its action because of what the charts are saying.

All charts are based on the principle of recording price movements over a period of time. They usually involve the plotting of every move a market makes (a point and figure chart) or the daily range and closing price (a line and bar chart). Often the volume, open interest and, perhaps, relative strength index (a variable worked out on a formula involving price movements over a period of time) are also plotted.

Point and figure charts

A point and figure chart (see Figure 10.1) involves the recording of an 'O' for every downward move of a certain size and an 'X' for every upward move. The size of the move is variable, but would normally be, say, 10 cents/barrel on the crude markets, 1 dollar per tonne on the IPE gas oil contract and 0.25 cents/gallon on the NYMEX gasoline and heating oil contracts.

$/bbl					
17.00	x				
16.90	x	o		x	
16.80	x	o	x		x
16.70	x	o	x	o	x
16.60	x	c)	x	o	x
16.50	x	o		o	x
16.40	x			o	x
16.30				o	x
16.20				o	

10.1 Point and figure chart.

Once the size of the movement has been chosen, the points are plotted on the graph each time the market moves. For example, heating oil moves on the New York market using a 0.20 cents/gallon movement would be plotted as follows:

Sequence of trades	Action taken
78.00	starting point
78.10	none
78.30	x plotted
78.40	x plotted
78.65	x plotted
78.80	x plotted
78.60	o plotted
78.40	o plotted

There is no fixed time scale for a point and figure chart: it is market movement that determines entries on to the chart not time. Many traders will mark the first entry of each week and month with a letter or number for information purposes, but it makes no difference to the analysis.

Line and bar charts

The most common chart used in the analysis of oil markets is a line and bar chart (see Figure 10.2). In this, a vertical line is drawn to connect the high price of the day to the low price of the day, with a

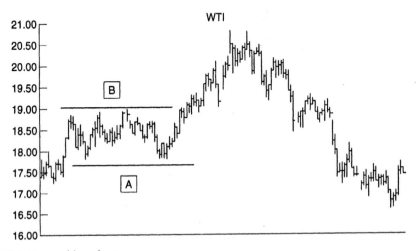

10.2 Line and bar chart.

horizontal bar to represent the closing price. Most commonly, one entry is made for each day and a chart such as is shown in this section is produced. Very short term traders, such as locals, are looking for intra-day trends and may use a five-minute line and bar chart, while those looking for longer term trends may use a weekly or even a monthly chart. The techniques of analysis are the same whatever the time scale.

Analysing the charts

The methods for analysing both of these charts are similar, though the line-and-bar chart is more popular and therefore used to illustrate the examples. Anyone interested in investigating technical analysis in depth will find a large number of detailed books on the subject, but for most users of the market a rudimentary understanding will suffice.

Support and resistance

The identification of support and resistance levels, where buying and selling respectively can be expected, is the first thing to look for. These come in three main types. The first is lateral support and resistance, where buying or selling repeatedly enters the market at the same price level. This gives a minimum buying price (support) (Figure 10.2-A) or maximum selling price (resistance) (Figure 10.2-B) in the current environment.

There are two types of trendline that can be constructed on price charts. An uptrend (Figure 10.3-A) connects the lows of the daily charts and a downtrend (B) connects the highs. All trendlines must touch three lows or highs. Once a trendline has been constructed it provides dynamic support and resistance. When prices return to the line, buying can be expected from an uptrend line and selling on a downtrend line. The absolute price at which the buying or selling will take place will change each day as the trendline is at a lower or higher price.

While the market continues to trade on one side of the line, the

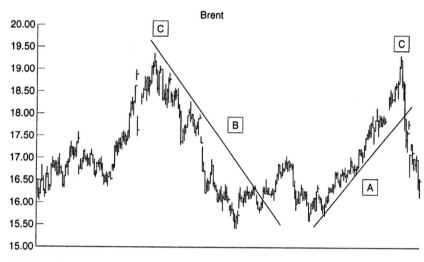

10.3 Trendlines.

trend can be expected to continue, but as soon as it closes on the other side the trend will be reversed. The technical trader may well move in and out of the market several times while a trend is in force, but will always play from the same side. Thus, in a downtrend, he will normally be short, though he may, from time to time, cover and then sell out again to take advantage of short term moves.

Once the market has reversed, the technical trader will close out existing positions but will not reverse them until a new trend has been formed, giving confirmation of the change of direction. In all charting methods, the top and bottom of a move will be missed, but the trend will not.

Finally, support and resistance will be found at previous highs and lows (C). This is another function of basic psychology: previous highs and lows provide reference points for traders who do not wish to pay higher or sell at lower prices than previously unless there is a very good reason.

Trendlines, support and resistance are all said to be broken when the market settles above resistance or below support. Frequently, the important levels will be broken during a day's trading but the market will close within the expected levels. In this case no action would be taken. But if support, resistance or a trendline are broken by the settlement or closing price a technical trader will say that the market has changed. If a market breaks up through resistance or a downtrend is broken a trader will close out any short positions and open a long one. If support or an uptrend are broken, long positions are closed and short ones taken.

Continuation patterns

Apart from basic support and resistance lines, technical analysts also look for continuation and reversal patterns. Continuation patterns suggest that a trend in force will continue while reversal patterns indicate that the trend has finished and will now be reversed. Flags and pennants are the simplest forms of continuation patterns. They are both indicative of a hesitation in an existing trend and usually mark the half-way point in a price move.

The target price given by the formation of a flag or pennant should be taken as an indicator rather than a definite target. It suggests that, with no major fundamental change, the market will continue until it reaches the target. But it may well continue beyond the target. Such a further move may be indicated by the formation of a further flag or pennant.

A flag (Figure 10.4) consists of two parallel trendlines sloping against the prevailing trend while a pennant (Figure 10.5) is two converging trendlines usually around the horizontal. Market activity normally declines as the formation is made. When prices break out of the flag or pennant, they can be expected to move as far up or down as they had before the pattern started.

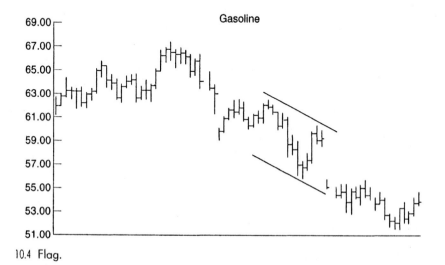

10.4 Flag.

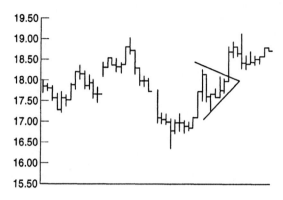

10.5 Pennant.

Reversal patterns

Reversal patterns are also an important part of technical analysis. It is important to remember that a reversal pattern is only significant if a trend is in existence. If prices are not in an existing trend, but perhaps are in a period of turbulence with no clear pattern emerging, reversal patterns may be seen but will not be significant.

All reversal patterns can be seen either at the top of an uptrend or at the bottom of a downtrend. Generally speaking, however, sharp reversals in price are less frequent at the end of a downtrend than they are at the end of an uptrend. This is because it is easier to destroy confidence in a market, and hence see falling prices, than it is to build it up after a slide in prices.

One pattern that is seen at the top or bottom of a trend is key reversal (Figure 10.6). In a key reversal in an uptrend the market

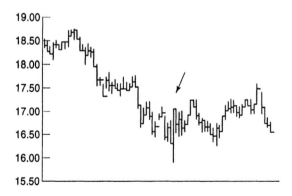

10.6 Key reversal.

makes a new high and then settles below the previous day's low. In a downtrend the market makes a new low and then settles above the previous day's high.

A similar pattern is the outside day reversal, where the line connecting the high and low is wholly outside the previous day's, i.e. there is a higher high and lower low than the previous day, but the market closes within the previous day's range. This is not as strong an indicator as the key reversal but often indicates a short term reversal in the trend, or correction.

Another reversal pattern is the head and shoulders, which despite its name can be seen at the top or bottom of the market. It is made up of several steps:

- Left shoulder – a rally in good volume followed by a dip
- Head – a rally to new highs in light volume followed by a dip
- Right shoulder – a rally in light volume to lower high
- Neckline – line connecting the two dips

Figure 10.7 shows a head and shoulders at the bottom of the market. The rules are the same in reverse, so there is a dip in price to the left shoulder (A), a short rally (B), then a new low forms the head (C), followed by another short rally (D). The right shoulder is formed by a third dip (E), which does not go as low as the head, and prices rally. The trend is broken when the market settles above the neckline (the line between B and D). The formation is completed when the market moves through the neckline after forming the right shoulder. Thus at

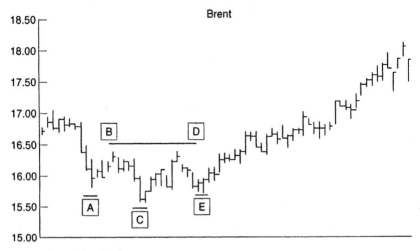

10.7 Head and shoulders.

the bottom of the market the reversal is confirmed when the market closes above the neckline and at the top when it closes below it.

Indicators

In addition to chart patterns the technical analyst will also use mathematical indicators, mainly designed to measure the momentum of the market. After the market has made a sharp move there will generally be a correction. This is not the same as a reversal: it is a short term change of direction mainly caused by profit-taking. For example, in an uptrend those who have bought speculatively at the beginning will decide to take profits and therefore sell the market. This depresses prices in the short term, but does not indicate a complete change of direction.

There are also a number of chart theories developed over the past 100 years or so. They are all designed to improve on the simple analysis of charts and to identify trends and changes in direction as early as possible. Any broker or a specialist would be able to explain the techniques further.

Two of the most common reversal patterns are double bottoms and double tops and head and shoulders (see above).

Figure 10.8 illustrates a double bottom. It is made up of four separate parts:

1. A fall in price
2. An upward reaction

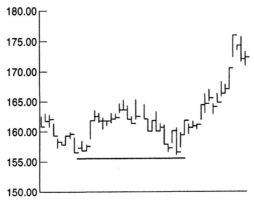

10.8 Double bottom.

3. A second fall to around the same level as the first
4. A second upward move

When the second upward move takes the price beyond the first rally a buy signal is given.

A double top is the reverse of this with a rally, a downward reaction, a second rally and a second fall to below the level of the first. This will give a sell signal.

Selecting stop levels

Another use of the charts is for determining support and resistance lines, frequently used to select stop levels. These are illustrated in Figure 10.2. A lateral support line is a horizontal (or virtually so) line drawn to join several lows while a resistance line connects highs. They therefore indicate the levels at which the market has halted previously and may well do so again. The more times a market bounces off a support or resistance line the stronger the reaction will be when it finally breaks through. If a market closes several times at around the same level, this can also be used as a measure of support or resistance.

As soon as a support or resistance line is broken it immediately changes its function. Thus, a broken support line becomes a resistance indication and vice versa.

Support and resistance lines are used to determine stop levels because they indicate that the market has moved out of the range previously traded. In New York particularly, this can result in a wave of selling orders triggered off as soon as the market touches a certain level. Any trader wishing to buy would therefore be advised to wait for some of these to come out and push the market down.

Moving average charts

Perhaps the most common charting method, and the foundation of many charting systems – as well as one of the simplest to understand – is the moving average chart. This is illustrated in Figure 10.9 a line and bar chart is plotted and various averages are overlaid. The most common are averages of the closing price, though highs, lows or combinations of all three may be used. At least two, usually three, moving averages are used in conjunction with the closing price to

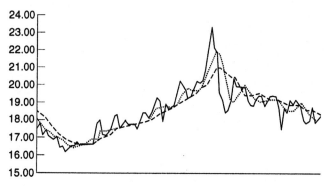

10.9 Closing price with 5- and 10-day moving averages.

indicate the strength or weakness of the market. Popular combinations include the 5, 10, 15 and 20-day averages, though 14, 18 and 19-day are also quite common.

Whatever averages are used, the principle of reading the chart is the same. A sell signal is given when the longest term average is above the next and so on with the close at the bottom. In the illustration the 10-day average is above the 5-day which is above the close. A buy signal is given when the three are in the reverse order: the close is above the 5-day which is above the 10-day.

Obviously the larger the number of days chosen for the longest-term average the longer the chart will take to change its indication. But if the averages are too short, they may turn before a trend has properly established itself.

The shorter term trends are used to determine that the market is still within the trend indicated by the longer term one. In all cases a trader is seeking to find the optimum combination which will give indication to a trend as quickly as possible without becoming too susceptible to short term fluctuations.

Gaps

A gap occurs on a chart when there is no overlap between one day's trading and the next, that is when the entire day's range is above the previous day's high or below the previous day's low. Markets generally try and fill gaps as soon as they are entered and both sides of a gap are significant because this demonstrates the strength or otherwise of the sentiment that led to the creation of the gap in the first place while the second provides an objective.

Technical indicators

There are a number of technical indicators used by technical traders. The most common is the relative strength index. The relative strength index (RSI) is used to determine whether a market is overbought or oversold. It is calculated over a period of days, most commonly nine days. Taking settlement price change (the difference between one day's close and the previous day's) for the last, say, nine days, the total upward move and downward move are calculated. The upward move is divided by the downward move and the result taken from a hundred. Thus a total upward move of 75 cents and downward move of 10 cents would give $(100 - 75/10) = 92.5$.

An RSI over 80 is usually considered to indicate an overbought market and an RSI below 20 an oversold one. The indicator shows that there are too many buyers in an overbought market, pushing the price up too high, while in an oversold market the downward moves are being overstressed.

As with all technical indicators, a change in the fundamentals of a contract will break the rules but the RSI is a useful indicator of the mood of the market. A very low RSI would indicate to a potential seller, for example, that he might want to wait a while before selling. It would not change his mind about whether to sell or not, but merely affect the timing.

Momentum indicators are also used extensively to monitor markets. There are a number of these used, probably the most common being the simple stochastic which calculates momentum from the closing price and its place in the recent trading range. It seeks to determine when a market is running out of enthusiasm for one directional move and is therefore likely to turn round.

There are also a large number of statistical and behavioural theories which have been developed over many years. These are of interest to those wanting to study charts in detail but are not for those who wish merely to have a rudimentary understanding of how the markets will be affected by charting theory.

Charts and the oil industry

It is unlikely that industry traders will trade entirely on the basis of technical analysis. Anyone with knowledge of the fundamentals is unlikely to be able to forget them and follow whatever the charts are saying regardless of the state of the physical market. None the less, all users of the market should have some understanding of what the various indications mean. Even if they do not look at charts themselves, their broker will certainly inform them of what the charts are saying and the volume of trading behind the charts makes them impossible to ignore; though ultimately, of course, the market will react to fundamentals.

It is also important to gain an understanding of what others in the markets are doing. Just as, for example, producers know the economics of refiners and so understand their buyers, so should those trading in the futures markets understand the activities of other users.

There are an enormous number of trading systems employed by brokers operating commodity funds. All of these are based on fairly simple charting techniques, as described here, with added refinements, mostly aimed at anticipating moves and therefore trading earlier than other systems. These funds have varying degrees of success and are an increasingly popular investment where tax laws are more favourable towards investors in commodities than they are in most European countries.

There is no magic about charts: some technical analysts describe them as maps. They identify trends, and will therefore be unsuccessful in a flat, drifting market with no clear direction or one with sharp fluctuations but no overall trend. By definition, they will miss the top and bottom of the market, but they should also iron out freak movements in price – when, for example, the market moves sharply on a rumour which turns out to be untrue.

Glossary of terms

ADP	Alternative delivery procedure, where delivery on the futures exchanges can be made outside the rules of the exchange by agreement between buyer and seller.
Arbitrage	The simultaneous purchase and sale of the same quantities of same or similar products in two different markets.
At-the-money	An option with a strike price at the current market price.
Backwardation	The price differential between two months when the nearer month is at a premium to the further one.
Basis	The difference in price between the futures or other derivative instrument and the physical price of the same crude or product.
Basis risk	The risk that the basis will change during the lifetime of a hedge.
Bear	One who thinks prices will fall.
Bid	(Futures) Commitment to buy one or more lots at the specified price.
Bull	One who thinks prices will rise.

Call option	An option giving the buyer the right to be long at the strike price.
Cap	A call option.
Cash market	Physical market.
CFD	Contract for difference. Any contract with financial settlement but normally used to describe the swap on the differential between dated Brent and the first forward month.
Clearing house	The agency with which all futures contracts are registered and which guarantees the performance of all contracts.
Collar	An option trade involving the purchase of calls and sale of puts or purchase of puts and sale of calls.
Contango	The price differential between two months when the nearer month is at a discount to the further one.
Dated Brent	A Brent cargo which has been nominated to the buyer for a specific loading range.
Declaration date	The day on which an option expires.
Delta	The amount by which an option premium changes with the underlying commodity price.
EFP	Exchange for physical. A physical deal priced on the futures market.
EFS	Exchange for a swap. A swap priced on the futures market.
Exercise	The conversion of an option to the underlying futures contract or other instrument.
Expiry date	The day on which an option expires.
Floor	A put option.
Forward market	A market dealing in contracts for future delivery.
Good-till-cancelled	An order which remains in the market until it is filled, instead of being cancelled at the end of the day.
Granter	The seller of an option.
Hedge	Taking an equal and opposite position with futures or another instrument to the physical position held.
Historical volatility	The statistical measure of the volatility of a market.

Implied volatility	The volatility of the market as determined from the option premium.
In-the-money	An option which would be profitable if exercised immediately.
Intrinsic value	The amount by which an option is in-the-money.
Last trading day	The last day of trading for a futures contract.
Liquidation	The closing of an existing position on any market.
Liquid market	A market in which users can trade the volume they wish without moving the price.
Long	Someone who has bought futures.
Lot	A standard contract unit.
Margin (original)	The returnable deposit charged by the clearing house when a position is opened.
Margin (variation)	The difference in value between the price at which the contract was opened and the current market value.
Mark to market	The process of re-valuing all futures contracts at the settlement price each day.
Market maker	1. A company providing over-the-counter instruments. 2. A company on the exchange options floors quoting all options.
Market order	An order to buy futures at whatever is the prevailing price.
Offer	(Futures) Commitment to sell one or more lots at the specified price.
Open position	The number of unclosed contracts on the futures market.
Option	An instrument giving the buyer the right to be long (a call option) or short (a put option) of a commodity at the strike price.
Out-of-the-money	An option which would not be profitable if exercised immediately.
Partial	A part-cargo of Brent or Dubai.
Premium	The amount paid by the buyer of an option.
Put option	An option giving the buyer the right to be short at the strike price.
Settlement price	The price at which the futures market closes. It is a weighted average of the last minute or two

	(depending on the market) of trading and is the price at which all futures contracts are margined.
Short	Someone who has sold futures.
Spot month	The nearest traded futures month.
Spread	The differential in price between two different contracts, whether in the same or different markets.
Stop order	An order to trade futures which becomes a market order as soon as the contract trades at a specified price. (Often used to limit losses, when it is known as a stop loss order.)
Strike price	The price at which an option may be exercised.
Swap	The exchange of a fixed price now for a floating price at a pre-determined time in the future.
Swaption	An option on swap contract.
Taker	The buyer of an option.
Time value	The part of an option value reflecting the time left to expiry (often also used to include all aspects of an option value except intrinsic value).
Trigger pricing	A deal allowing the buyer or seller to choose when to fix the price of a deal on several occasions.
Writer	The seller of an option.

Appendix

Costs of futures trading

There are three basic components in the costs of futures trading: initial margins, variation margins and commissions. Of these, the first is fixed by the clearing house, with reference to the exchange, the second is dependent on the price movement in the market and the third is negotiated with the broker.

Initial margins are payable as soon as a futures position is opened. They are fixed by the clearing house and vary according to the volatility of the market. They are normally equivalent to 5–10 per cent of the total contract value, but can be varied at any time without notice if volatility changes. The clearing houses allow market users to use treasury bills or certain other securities to fund initial margins or pay interest if they are paid in cash. They are returned as soon as the position is closed. They are part of the means by which the clearing house is able to guarantee the contract.

On most markets, initial margins are increased as a contract nears expiry. They can also be varied for some members of the market but not all. Initial margins are reduced for spread positions.

The other part of the guarantee system is the variation margins.

These are payable on a daily basis according to price movement in the market. Each night all contracts are marked to market: this means that they are revalued at the settlement price. Thus a contract may have been bought during the day at, say, $20.00/bbl and the market closes at $20.10/bbl. The contract is now revalued and the buyer is long at $20.10/bbl and receives 10 cents/bbl from the clearing house. If the following day prices fall to $19.90/bbl the position is revalued again and the buyer is long at $19.90/bbl. Variation margins must be paid in cash.

The commissions payable are entirely a matter of negotiation between broker and client. They will depend on the level of service required and the volume of business being done. Commissions can also be affected by any financial arrangements between broker and client, such as credit agreements.

There are fees payable to the exchange and the clearing house for every lot traded on a futures market. These are paid by the executing broker to the exchange and the clearing member to the clearing house. Some brokers will quote commissions including these fees and others will quote two figures.

Index

Printed in the United Kingdom
by Lightning Source UK Ltd.
111409UKS00001B/85-132